New Directions for
Higher Education

Martin Kramer and
Judith Block McLaughlin
CO-EDITORS-IN-CHIEF

W9-AHR-901

Practical Approaches to Ethics for Colleges and Universities

Stephanie L. Moore

EDITOR

Number 142 • Summer 2008
Jossey-Bass
San Francisco

PRACTICAL APPROACHES TO ETHICS FOR COLLEGES AND UNIVERSITIES
Stephanie L. Moore (ed.)
New Directions for Higher Education, no. 142
Martin Kramer, Judith Block McLaughlin, Co-Editors-in-Chief

Microfilm copies of issues and articles are available in 16mm and 35mm, as well as microfiche in 105mm, through University Microfilms Inc., 300 North Zeeb Road, Ann Arbor, Michigan 48106-1346.

NEW DIRECTIONS FOR HIGHER EDUCATION (ISSN 0271-0560, electronic ISSN 1536-0741) is part of The Jossey-Bass Higher and Adult Education Series and is published quarterly by Wiley Subscription Services, Inc., A Wiley Company, at Jossey-Bass, 989 Market Street, San Francisco, California 94103-1741. Periodicals Postage Paid at San Francisco, California, and at additional mailing offices. POSTMASTER: Send address changes to New Directions for Higher Education, Jossey-Bass, 989 Market Street, San Francisco, California 94103-1741.

New Directions for Higher Education is indexed in Current Index to Journals in Education (ERIC); Higher Education Abstracts.

SUBSCRIPTIONS cost $85 for individuals and $209 for institutions, agencies, and libraries. See ordering information page at end of journal.

EDITORIAL CORRESPONDENCE should be sent to the Co-Editors-in-Chief, Martin Kramer, 2807 Shasta Road, Berkeley, California 94708-2011 and Judith Block McLaughlin, Harvard GSE, Gutman 435, Cambridge, Massachusetts 02138.

Cover photograph © Digital Vision

www.josseybass.com

CONTENTS

EDITOR'S NOTES

Nailing Mud: A Practical Approach to Ethics for Institutions of Higher Education

Ethics. Just the mention probably makes you want to find something else to do. Although we know ethics are critical and often are a large part of poor employee or organizational performance, we're also not quite sure how to tackle a topic that seems so full of variability, contradicting viewpoints, and squishy definitions. As Matchett (in this issue) notes, many discussions on ethics tend to devolve into a muddy pool of individual beliefs and values, personal preferences, and unreflective relativistic conclusions. As a result, we wind up in an unfortunate, unintended wasteland between knowing we should address the topic but not quite knowing how, and therefore leaving (or pushing) it aside.

To borrow and modify the argument from William McDonough, an engineer and sustainability expert, it's simply no longer acceptable for us to say this isn't part of our plan (2006). Ethical outcomes are part of our *de facto* plan. Whether we consciously plan for ethical outcomes or not, they happen. We teach implicit lessons on ethics; we model ethical (or unethical) behavior or reasoning, often unconsciously; and our practices deliver certain results, both to students and employees as well as to society. What we as universities and university employees do, deliver, and produce has an impact. If we do not plan for desired impact, we can become "strategically tragic"—delivering undesirable consequences to the external world and society and to those internal to the university whom we serve as well (students and employees).

As the import of this topic is increasingly highlighted, even becoming a desired characteristic of the students a university graduates (Procario-Foley and Bean, 2002; Hammond, 1992, cited in Dean, 1993), universities are involved (whether they actively participate or not) in a growing discussion of ethics to include topics such as socially responsible practices of universities, professional ethics, research ethics, ethical competencies, curricular integration, and teaching strategies. It is a discussion with many layers of complexity. In this special issue on ethics in higher education, we look at the layers of complexity. This issue has been specifically constructed to look at ethics in higher education all the way from strategic planning and purpose of educational institutions into major operational aspects across universities, such as research, educational and information technologies, and sustainability, and on down into integration of ethics into curricula, specific implications for subsets of learners such as business majors, diverse student populations, or student-athletes, and then on down even into classroom strategies. Whether you

NEW DIRECTIONS FOR HIGHER EDUCATION, no. 142, Summer 2008 © Wiley Periodicals, Inc.
Published online in Wiley InterScience (www.interscience.wiley.com) • DOI: 10.1002/he.298

are an administrator, faculty member, new or experienced researcher, nonacademic department manager, or a student, the layers of this issue have been specifically selected and arranged to meet you where you are within your university. Thus begins the process of nailing mud.

With this issue, we move from assumptive or uncoordinated approaches to ethics into models for conscious, coordinated (or deliberate) efforts. Indeed, all good planning, whether it's institutional planning or instructional planning or research planning, begins with a deliberate, considered articulation of the desired results. It is only through this conscious consideration and clear articulation that we can begin to move. But just *moving* isn't enough; we can plan to move in a desired direction to accomplish desired ends (the difference between *moving* and *movement*).

Within institutions of higher education, we can plan at different levels. We tend to jump to curriculum and courses, because these are the familiar processes and products of a university. They are important, but we can miss the forest for the trees if we address ethics only at that level. Ethics start by thinking outside of ourselves. Thus, we begin by situating higher education within the larger whole, by thinking outside ourselves to consider on whom and what we have an impact—a systemic framework for thinking and planning.

Systemic Thinking: Higher Education as a Part of the Whole

Most of the tradition of ethics may be said to focus on the individual, whether it is individual choices, individual moral reasoning, individual character, or individual differences. However, a new paradigm for thinking about human relations has ushered in a whole new set of frameworks, theories, models, research insights, and so forth. The new paradigm is systems thinking, derived from General System Theory, first proposed by von Bertalanffy (1951, 1968). The systemic framework emphasizes the interrelated, interconnected nature of everything; what I do here ripples out and has an effect there. As diffusion of innovation researcher Rogers (2003) expressed it, when you move a marble in a bowl, it causes the other marbles to shift.

Ethics as expressed in this issue are focused on the impact of your marble on other marbles—whether it's the impact of the university as a whole or individual researchers and graduates on society, the impact of subsystems in the university on people within, or the impact of the institution or teachers on students. This issue has been constructed from a systemic framework, focusing on the university both as a whole and as part of a whole.

Systemically speaking, our colleges and universities are part of the larger whole of society. Thus, the work of an institution of higher education is interconnected with society at large. Whether we acknowledge that relationship or not, it exists and we have desirable or undesirable impact on the world around us. As Dale Brethower states, we are either adding or subtracting value (2006). It is up to us to decide what value we add or want to add and plan toward that. Kaufman asserts:

> The simple truth is that what the schools do and what the schools accomplish is of concern to those who depend upon the schools, those who pay the bills and those who pass the legislation. We are not in a vacuum, and our results are seen and judged by those outside of the schools—those who are external to it. . . . This external referent should be the starting place for functional and useful educational planning, design, implementation, and evaluations—if education does not allow learners to live better and contribute better, it probably is not worth doing, and will probably end up being attacked and decimated by taxpayers and legislators [1996, p. 112].

Within our walls, colleges and universities are also self-contained wholes. We have many parts to the system that all add up to the whole university or whole college system. From administration to facilities and operations, to budget and dining, to student services and faculty, and of course, the students—there are many moving parts. A change in one area will necessarily affect the other area, and ethical considerations involve a conscious articulation of what the desired effect should be. Indeed, many of the questions over ethics and how to address them arise within the organization.

One significant aspect to higher education's relationship with the whole is the societal expectation of what we deliver, namely via our graduates. As numerous professions faced public ethical failures that led to criticisms of the professions and revised curricula, more attention has been turned to higher education as the home for ethical considerations across disciplines. Let's examine some of the driving forces for this societal change and then explore why higher education has such a significant role to play.

Driving Forces for Ethics in Higher Education

Davis (1999) describes what he calls an "ethics boom" in higher education during the past thirty years, where one by one professions have been faced with a requirement to integrate ethics explicitly in university programs. Technological advances, national scandals, and poor performance have driven other professions to build ethics into college curriculum as a means of ensuring good decision making and defining standards for members of a profession.

The medical profession was among the first to see a need for ethics integration into college curricula (Davis, 1999). Advances in medical technology confronted practicing physicians with difficult decisions, as they had to choose what deserved budget allocations. Though one machine could save the lives of a few dozen patients, the equipment was so expensive that the same amount of money could also build an outpatient clinic that would serve many more people but not save lives. Technology also changed the practice of medicine, as house calls grew increasingly impractical and physicians no longer had a sense of personal relationship with patients. To address these issues directly in practice and train the next generation of physicians for these decisions, the medical community turned to philosophy departments to help them build courses on practical ethics. However, philosophy focused on moral theories, not applied ethics. At a few universities, philosophers and physicians agreed to work together, and as parties from both sides talked more, philosophers realized that ethical issues in the medical field related directly to traditional topics in philosophy courses. Davis (1999) explains that by the late 1960s, this conversation had advanced enough to become institutionalized. Several centers arose, courses on medical ethics became common in all the leading universities across the country, and the first textbook on medical ethics was published in 1976 (Davis, 1999).

The driving force for ethics in the legal profession was quite different. When it became a public point of embarrassment that many of President Richard Nixon's team members involved in the criminal activities of Watergate were lawyers, the legal profession faced public demand for ethics in their practices and training. Some states started requiring ethics courses as a condition for admission to the bar; other states quickly followed suit, and law schools suddenly found themselves facing social and legal requirements to teach ethics to their students (Davis, 1999). Davis states that the law profession was a little different from the medical field because the law literature had developed ethical concepts. However, they were still caught in the same problem of definition: How do codes of ethics translate into professional responsibilities and performance standards? As the profession grappled with distinctions, courses on ethics in major national programs became the norm and remain a staple requirement today.

Soon, the typical cluster of engineering and science disciplines followed suit with the legal and medical professions. Spiro Agnew, Richard Nixon's vice president, had resigned office because of a bribing scandal involving a number of engineers during his office term in Maryland. Civil engineers seeking state contracts had bribed Agnew to obtain those contracts. When news spread, "Engineers all over the country were appalled that so many engineers could be involved in such a flagrant violation of professional ethics" (Davis, 1999, p. 7). Davis explains that engineers were already uneasy because their field had been involved in fake testing on Goodrich's A-7D airbrakes, the Ford Pinto's exploding gas tank, and the DC-10's misdesigned cargo door. Furthermore, engineers were aware that fellow professionals who raised questions about adverse social impacts, such as environmental hazards, were losing their positions. In light of these issues, in 1975 an ethics center was established to address ethics in engineering, architecture, science, and related fields. Development of courses in engineering ethics followed the same pattern as the legal and medical fields, partnering with philosophy departments to highlight topics and issues and develop courses that became required components of the curricula (Davis, 1999).

From this period forward, many disciplines started following the same pattern: business, accounting, nursing, journalism, financial analysis, public administration, dentistry, and others. The trend is clearly toward deep integration of ethics into college curricula, specialized to each discipline (Davis, 1999). Frankel (1989) explains that in the recent past, discussion on professional ethics occurred only within the professions themselves. Historically, professions have maintained a negotiating process with society, keeping a tension between the autonomy of a profession to define and regulate itself and the public's demand for accountability. Frankel states, "Society's granting of power and privilege to the professions is premised on their willingness and ability to contribute to social well-being and to conduct their affairs in a manner consistent with broader social values" (p. 110).

Higher Education: The Place for Ethics Development

Clearly, as ethical issues were identified and as ethical decision making was studied, professions have turned to higher education programs as the place for training members in their profession on professional ethics. The role of ethics in professional education has long been noted as essential, even stemming back to Socrates, who said that no craft or profession should seek its own advantage but should benefit those who are subject to it (Baumgarten, 1982). Baumgarten argues that, through university teaching, "we express our conviction that thoughtful inquiry ennobles a human life and contributes to human excellence . . . there is special reason to value a profession that is solely committed to enlarging the power and influence of reason discourse and imaginative questioning" (p. 294).

Speaking more specifically to technical professions, Davis (1993) states that professional ethics are different from ordinary ethics in that they cannot be learned in families, religious institutions, or primary or secondary schools. Professional ethics pertain to members of a particular profession, and entrance into that profession is gained only through some form of advanced study. Thus, the place of advanced study is the very place where professional ethics must be learned, either as a formal part of the education or in some less formal way in job settings. Davis points out that in recent years, consensus developed in technical disciplines that professional schools were not doing enough to teach professional ethics. For example, accrediting bodies began adding requirements that ethics be a part of the curriculum (see *Criteria for Accrediting Programs in Engineering in the United States [1989–90 Academic Year]*, sec. IV.C.2.i., New York, Accreditation Board of Engineering and Technology, pp. 8-9, as cited in Davis, 1993, p. 231).

NEW DIRECTIONS FOR HIGHER EDUCATION • DOI: 10.1002/he

Furthermore, universities are viewed as the place where training in ethics should take place prior to graduates entering the workforce. Procario-Foley and Bean (2002) argue that organizations require recruitment of "graduates who have world-class ethics to accompany their world-class knowledge" (p. 105).Indeed, this reflects recent findings that more than 60 percent of organizations rank ethics as one of the top priorities they look for in candidates for open positions (Hammond, 1992; cited in Dean, 1993).Caron (1999) urges that higher education institutions are in a unique position to train graduates on how to address social concerns without having to adopt any particular political agenda, and they can do so with intellectual rigor and professional capacity.

Finally, research indicates that the ethical philosophies and values (and resulting behaviors) of management or leaders influence ethical choices and behaviors of employees and other organizational members (Brenner and Molander, 1977; Ford and Richardson, 1994; Petrick and Quinn, 1997; Procario-Foley and Bean, 2002).We can translate the language of business to education programs, where faculty in leadership and mentorship positions model philosophies and behaviors that may influence students—who become future faculty, practitioners, or researchers—in their programs. O'Connell (1998) proposes, "Our task in universities is not only to teach ethics and values for the marketplace but to model these values ourselves as we fulfill our own moral responsibility as educators in the universities where our students begin the business ethics journey in the first place" (p. 1620). Procario-Foley and Bean (2002) explain that students are keenly aware of the ethical behaviors their course instructors demonstrate. They write, "Teaching faculty are exemplars for students and it is essential that they reflect and personify the values of the institution" (p. 112). Thus, college programs are the place where professional ethics are both taught and modeled, on a practical day-to-day basis. If change in ethical awareness and behavior is to happen, it will come from the degree programs and institutions themselves.

We start with ethics in the strategic planning process and overall design and intent of any given educational institution, and then drill down into deeper layers of universities to look at a variety of topics. In truth, for ethics to truly be present, it must be present at all levels of a university, as a conscious effort rather than one that is assumed. Some articles in this issue address ways in which higher education and individual institutions are a part of the whole and how we can plan toward desirable social results. Other articles address the parts of the university system, looking at how the value a university adds—to people without and people within—flows down into university operations and processes.

One of the biggest barriers to integration of ethics is that most faculty and staff do not feel comfortable with the content area (Davis, 1993). Many faculty believe that because they were not philosophy majors or are not content experts on ethics, that they are not equipped to teach ethics (or worry that they might even be dangerous because they know little about it). It is the hope of all the authors in this issue that each piece makes ethics approachable and practical, elucidating just how they can be taught and practiced throughout the entire university system, regardless of whether you have studied ethics or this is the first piece on ethics you have ever read. Many of us are other-content experts first, with a diverse set of roles and functions within our universities. We invite you to share in how we have tackled ethics in a meaningful, practical way.

Stephanie L. Moore
Editor

References

Baumgarten, E. "Ethics in the Academic Profession." *Journal of Higher Education*, 1982, 53(3), 282–295.

Brenner, S. N., and Molander, E. "Is the Ethics of Business Changing?" *Harvard Business Review*, 1977, 5(1), 57–71.

Brethower, D. *Performance Analysis: Knowing What to Do and How*. Amherst, Mass.: HRD Press, 2006.

Caron, B. (ed.). *Service Matters: The Engaged Campus*. Providence, R.I.: Campus Compact, 1999.

Davis, M. "Ethics Across the Curriculum: Teaching Professional Responsibility in Technical Courses." *Teaching Philosophy*, 1993, 16(3), 205–235.

Davis, M. *Ethics and the University*. London: Routledge, 1999.

Dean, P. J. "A Selected Review of the Underpinnings of Ethics for Human Performance Technology Professionals—Part One: Key Ethical Theories and Research." *Performance Improvement Quarterly*, 1993, 6(4), 3–32.

Ford, R., and Richardson, W. "Ethical Decision Making: A Review of the Empirical Literature." *Journal of Business Ethics*, 1994, 13, 205–221.

Frankel, M. "Professional Codes: Why, How, and With What Impact?" *Journal of Business Ethics*, 1989, 8, 109–115.

Kaufman, R. "Needs Assessment: Internal and External." In D. Ely and T. Plomp (eds.), *Classic Writings on Instructional Technology*. Englewood, Colo.: Libraries Unlimited, 1996.

McDonough, W. "Cradle to Cradle Design." Retrieved Dec. 3, 2006 from iTunes, Stanford series (accessed Jan. 15, 2008).

O'Connell, D. W. "From the Universities to the Marketplace: The Business Ethics Journey." *Journal of Business Ethics*, 1998, 17, 1617–1622.

Petrick, J., and Quinn, J. *Management Ethics: Integrity at Work*. Thousand Oaks, Calif.: Sage, 1997.

Procario-Foley, E., and Bean, D. "Institutions of Higher Education: Cornerstones in Building Ethical Organizations." *Teaching Business Ethics*, 2002, 6, 101–116.

Rogers, E. *Diffusion of Innovations* (5th ed). New York: Free Press, 2003.

von Bertalanffy, L. "General System Theory: A New Approach to Unity of Science." *Human Biology*, Dec. 1951, 23, 303–361.

von Bertalanffy, L. *General System Theory: Foundations, Development, Applications*. New York: Braziller, 1968.

1

Ethics as part of strategic planning are about adding measurable value to our shared world, not just talking about doing the right things.

A Practical Definition of Ethics for Truly Strategic Planning in Higher Education

Roger Kaufman

Every one of us is headed to the same place. All of us. It doesn't make any difference what race, color, creed, gender, religion, or national origin we individually represent. It doesn't make any difference if we are political leftists, liberals, right-wingers, conservatives, or neutral. We are all headed to the same place. It doesn't make any difference if we are learners or teachers, or what our age.

We are all headed to the same place: the future.

Given this, doesn't it make sense to be very clear about that future? Does it not make additional sense to ensure that the future has positive consequences for each and every one of us? If someone's future is poverty and petulance, none of us really benefit. If it is terror or ignorance, none of us benefit. It is to our mutual advantage for everyone to make decisions that result in consequences that will add measurable value to our individual and collective well-being. This forms the basis for a suggested definition of ethics, a social-benefit definition. This suggested definition applies to education as well as any other type of human organization, and to our shared world.

On the surface, it appears that educational institutions are attending to this humanistic orientation; the rhetoric of education is about making life better for people. However, an assumption that your institution is actually having the desired impact is just that: an assumption. In any organization, no matter its stated intentions to add value to our shared society, the results and impacts can and should be measured in order to demonstrate the value

NEW DIRECTIONS FOR HIGHER EDUCATION, no. 142, Summer 2008   © Wiley Periodicals, Inc.
Published online in Wiley InterScience (www.interscience.wiley.com) • DOI: 10.1002/he.299

the institution and all its parts add to society. Adding measurable value to our shared world is what every organization must deliver. Thus, we start with a *practical* definition of ethics that can be used for strategic planning in an educational institution. From this perspective, ethics become something you *do* as an organization, not just something you say.

Some History of This Approach

Ethics. What a messy topic. The word may elicit responses ranging from "doing things right" (as proposed by the National Education Association in 1975, when it advocated treating each learner with dignity and understanding individual differences) to "doing the right things" that deliver useful results—the guide offered by Peter Drucker (1973, 1985, 1988, 1992, 1993).

As a humbling effort, Google the term *ethics*. Definitions from scholars, observers, and interested parties generally move in a "process direction" that advises organizations to treat people with respect, dignity, and honesty. Few definitions look are in terms of the measurable and quantifiable results that "ethics" applied usefully will deliver. To save the reader the anguish of sorting through Googled "ethics," definitions, and discussions, Moore in her 2005 unpublished doctoral dissertation on ethics as considered in educational technology offers a comprehensive review of the literature on higher education.

I am results-and-consequences-biased, so my satisfaction with the "doing things right" approach moves me toward a "get the right things accomplished" and measurable value added consequences mode. So the journey to define ethics in terms of consequences and not in terms of process begins. The first part of the journey is to look not at ethical processes but ethical consequences.

I have researched and propose a framework and definition for useful societal value added (cf. Kaufman, 1992, 1998, 2000, 2006a, 2006b). This framework has been used in government organizations, the military (including international militaries), large corporations around the globe, and educational institutions such as the Sonora Institute for Technology in Sonora, Mexico. This framework is termed an "Ideal Vision"—defined more fully in an example data collection instrument to calibrate the results of ethical decisions given below—that expresses societal value added in terms of related variables. Taken together, these elements of an Ideal Vision will offer a useful definition of *ethics* generally and in education specifically.

The elements of this suggested Ideal Vision (I use this term to also mean Mega-level planning and outcomes) are presented here to furnish a useful definition of "ethics." Given some of the atrocious things that have been done under the label of "visions" and "visioning," some people recoil from the term. In those cases, I use the term *vital signs* for any organization to use in terms of what it commits to deliver to our shared world.

These elements or dimensions of the Ideal Vision are given below in a vehicle for defining "ethics in education." They constitute a platform for validation and revision. For my current thinking, "ethics in education" is based on decisions and actions that lead to a situation where all citizens survive and have a positive quality of life. It is the responsibility of every citizen and every organization, public and private, to add value to all other citizens and residents of our shared world. Thus, ethics are what lead to decisions that guide us to the measurable value added for all stakeholders.

To briefly demonstrate how we might move toward a more functional definition of ethics, here is a draft exercise intended for data collection. This exercise allows one or one's institution to identify the elements of ethics (including ethics in education) and develop a personal as well as organizational articulation of possible contributions to society at large.

Identifying an Organization's Current Contribution to Practical Ethics in Education

This sample data collection framework is based on the elements of an Ideal Vision (Kaufman, 1998, 2000, 2006a, 2006b; Kaufman, Oakley-Browne, Watkins, and Leigh, 2003; Kaufman and Guerra-Lopez, 2008). An Ideal Vision has been derived by asking people almost worldwide to define, in measurable terms, the kind of world they would want to create for tomorrow's children. This has been done relatively informally in many international settings and contexts. The responses are impressively similar. What has evolved from content analyses of these responses to "what kind of world would you like to create for your children and grandchildren?" has inspired me to call this "mother's rule," because it is the results-referenced perceptions that most women would hold relative to future generations.

Thus, an Ideal Vision encompasses a measurable set of statements about where people and organizations are headed and defines why they want to get there and how to tell when they have arrived. This definition is the heart of ethics—decisions that lead to this continuous improvement for all stakeholders.

As an exercise, individuals or organizations may identify the various elements (suggested here as the elements of ethics) and identify the gaps between their ethical decisions and what they think should be their ethical decisions. The elements of the Ideal Vision are broken into cluster elements. Respondents then identify, on a five-point scale, the extent to which they and their organization currently add value to each element. The approach would then ask the sample to identify the extent to which it *should* add value in each area and its positive impact for external clients and our shared society. For each of the basic elements of an Ideal Vision, the respondents check if their organization currently makes a contribution to that element and thus to the total Ideal Vision. For each element of an Ideal Vision, respondents check terms of a rating scale running from (1) definitely to (5) definitely not.

This is an excellent opportunity, in educational institutions in particular, to stop and think consciously about just what our institutions impact. Using this framework, an institution can have a guided discussion on just what it does or does not impact and what it could and should (Table 1.1).

Thus any organization, including governments, can calibrate the equity of results for various stakeholders. Taken together, this also defines ethics as applied to decision making to add value to each other and our shared society. By identifying what contributions your institution makes to society, you articulate the specific, unique value your institution adds to society.

One is acting ethically when one's decisions are made on the basis of the consequences of any decision, public or private—checking whether those decisions add value to each other and our shared society. As Dale Brethower notes (2006), "If you are not adding value to society, you are subtracting value."

By starting with these criteria for desired societal consequences, you can then strategically plan for your institution to deliver the desired results. By doing so, ethics become a core part of the very *doing* of your institution. Ethics are no longer a document in the archives but a strategic plan of action for ensuring your institution adds value to society (locally and globally). Society likes organizations that deliver a benefit, and it keeps these organizations funded or in business over the long run because of the actual, measurable benefit being delivered. Thus, by integrating this approach into your strategic planning process, you are moving your institution in a direction that looks at long-term sustainability and viability. This sort of strategic planning is called Mega planning (Kaufman, 2000, 2006a, 2006b).

A very quick calibration for decision making, based on the Ideal Vision, is, "Will this bring us closer or farther away from Mega?" (Mega is the set of measurable contributions we just covered). An advantage if one applies this definition is that we can simplify and clarify the differences between politics (where *who* is more important than *what*, ranging from politics at the schoolhouse to the White House, and from international decisions to individual survival) and positive quality of life.

A warning: no approach is immune to bias, stereotypes, and confusing means and ends. Any approach that does not align individual results with organizational results with societal impacts cannot deal with such a definition of ethics as offered here. Distortion is a potent antidote to this approach. Of course, rationalizations abound: "My organization won't let me do this" and "I just do what I am told" and "No one does this now; why

Table 1.1. Measurable Value-Added Results Your Institution Delivers to Society

Basic Ideal Vision Elements: *There will be no loss of life or elimination of the survival of any species required for human survival. There will be no reduction in levels of self-sufficiency, quality of life livelihood, or loss of property from any source, including:*	Makes a contribution (1 = none 5 = completely):		
	Now 1 2 3 4 5	Should 1 2 3 4 5	Gap 1 2 3 4 5
War, riot, or terrorism			
Shelter			
Unintended human-caused changes to the environment, including permanent destruction of the environment or rendering it nonrenewable			
Murder, rape, or crimes of violence, robbery, or destruction of property			
Substance abuse			
Disease			
Pollution			
Starvation or malnutrition			
Child abuse			
Partner or spouse abuse			
Accidents, including transportation, home, and business or workplace			
Consequences: No adult will be under the care, custody, or control of another person, agency, or substance; all adult citizens will be self-sufficient and self-reliant as minimally indicated by their consumption being equal to or less than their production.			
Poverty will not exist, and every woman and man will earn as least as much as it costs them to live unless they are progressing toward being self-sufficient and self-reliant			

should I?" For those, I would simply ask, "Is that the way you want others to make ethical decisions?"

This may not be the way others do business now, but it is the way you can choose for your institution to do business.

So we start with ethics for educational institutions at the strategic planning level: How do you drive your organization in a direction that delivers

New Directions for Higher Education • DOI: 10.1002/he

measurable, desirable societal results? This article has explained the general framework for practical ethics applied at the strategic planning level in educational organizations. From there, ethics can be integrated down into the processes and parts of the institution, but those will be valuable only insofar as your institution cleasrly articulates what results it chooses to deliver to society.

Some possible ethical questions for education:

1. Is the curriculum leading to societal value-added? How do we know?
2. Is subject matter coverage sufficient for education to believe we are adding value to our learners and our shared world? If yes, what subject matter do we select, and how do we know what to continue, what to change, and what to delete?
3. Does what we use, do, produce, and deliver meet any objective criteria for adding value to our shared world?
4. Do we relate choice and consequences for learners, educators, parents, communities, organizations, and society?
5. Do the incentives we offer our educational partners lead to performance and consequences for Mega and societal value-added for all?

Summary

This proposed definition of "applied ethics" identifies an effort to delineate the framework and measurable indicators for positive-purpose-driven ethics regardless of the organizational context.

By applying the framework of an Ideal Vision (Mega) to the definition of "ethics," we may begin a dialogue with scholars and practitioners concerning what is ethics and how we might define it and evaluate what progress we are making. The rigorous definition for ethics will help obtain commitment to moving ever closer to it. If we cannot define and agree on what ethics in education is, we cannot plan for its achievement. If we are not planning for its achievement, then our de facto plan is for its demise.

References

Brethower, D. *Performance Analysis: Knowing What to Do and How.* Amherst, Mass.: HRD Press, 2006.

Drucker, P. F. *Management: Tasks, Responsibilities, Practices.* New York: Harper and Row, 1973.

Drucker, P. F. *Innovation and Entrepreneurship.* London: Heinemann, 1985.

Drucker, P. F. "Management and the World's Work." *Harvard Business Review,* 1988, 66(5), 65–76.

Drucker, P. F. "The New Society of Organizations." *Harvard Business Review,* 1992, 70(5), 95–104.

Drucker, P. F. *Post-Capitalist Society.* New York: HarperBusiness, 1993.

Kaufman, R. *Strategic Planning Plus: An Organizational Guide* (Rev. ed.). Thousand Oaks, Calif.: Sage, 1992.

Kaufman, R. *Strategic Thinking: A Guide to Identifying and Solving Problems* (Rev. ed.). Arlington, Va., and Washington, D.C.: jointly published by American Society for Training and Development and International Society for Performance Improvement, 1998.

Kaufman, R. *Mega Planning: Practical Tools for Organizational Success.* Thousand Oaks, Calif.: Sage, 2000.

Kaufman, R. *Change, Choices, and Consequences: A Guide to Mega Thinking and Planning.* Amherst, Mass.: HRD Press, 2006a.

Kaufman, R. *Thirty Seconds That Can Change Your Life: A Decision-Making Guide for Those Who Refuse to be Mediocre.* Amherst, Mass.: HRD Press, 2006b.

Kaufman, R., and Guerra-Lopez, I. *The Assessment Book: Applied Strategic Thinking and Performance Improvement Through Self-Assessments.* Amherst, Mass.: HRD Press, 2008.

Kaufman, R., Oakley-Browne, H., Watkins, R., and Leigh, D. *Strategic Planning for Success: Aligning People, Performance, and Payoff.* San Francisco: Jossey-Bass/Pfeiffer, 2003.

Moore, S. L. *The Social Impact of a Profession: An Analysis of Factors Influencing Ethics and the Teaching of Social Responsibility in Educational Technology Programs.* Unpublished doctoral dissertation, College of Education, University of Northern Colorado, 2005.

National Education Association. "Code of Ethics of the Education Profession," 1975. Retrieved Apr. 12, 2008, http://www.nea.org/aboutnea/code.html.

ROGER KAUFMAN is professor emeritus, Florida State University, director of Roger Kaufman and Associates, and distinguished research professor at the Sonora Institute of Technology, Mexico. He has published thirty-nine books and more than 250 articles on strategic planning, performance improvement, quality management and continuous improvement, needs assessment, management, and evaluation. He consults worldwide. He may be contacted at rkaufman@nettally.com. Further tools for conducting strategic planning are available at www.e-valuate-it.com/instruments/rka.

2

The existing pedagogy known as service learning could be harnessed and expanded as a model by which to teach sustainability.

Service Learning as an Expression of Ethics

Julie Newman

The demonstrated willingness of institutions of higher education to contribute to sustainable development is on the rise. Colleges and universities are attempting to integrate principles of sustainability into their operational practices, curriculum, and research priorities. Integrating sustainability into a university requires processes by which to reconcile a shared vision of a sustainable institution with the complexity, abstraction, and depth as well as the moral and ethical implications that sustainability purports. An underlying driver of this movement is that the graduates of these institutions, regardless of discipline, will be forced to cope with unprecedented environmental circumstances. Students enrolled in two- and four-year degree programs will face a new set of local and global challenges on entrance into the workforce. University graduates will be challenged to stabilize world population, reduce the emission of greenhouse gases that induce climate change, assess and protect biological diversity, avert the destruction of forests worldwide, conserve energy, prevent soil erosion, develop new technologies, value carbon, protect our watersheds, reduce asthma related to air pollution, and build an economy that handles and eliminates waste while developing renewable technology (Orr, 1992). One way in which college graduates will become exposed to these global complexities is if their universities are prepared and willing to make difficult decisions and embrace the underlying principles of sustainable development. Orr (1994), a long-time advocate for sustainability education, succinctly stated: "The kind of education we need begins with the recognition that the crisis of global ecology is first and foremost a crisis of values, ideas, perspectives, and knowledge, which makes it a crisis *of* education, not one *in* education" (p. 5).

NEW DIRECTIONS FOR HIGHER EDUCATION, no. 142, Summer 2008 © Wiley Periodicals, Inc.
Published online in Wiley InterScience (www.interscience.wiley.com) • DOI: 10.1002/he.300

At the core of this challenge remains the fundamental question of how students will become exposed to these pressing issues and be educated to derive solutions.

The National Wildlife Federation issued a report titled the "National Report Card on Environmental Performance and Sustainability in Higher Education" (2001). The report findings suggested that a variety of educational models have been developed that include degree requirements and interdepartmental minors to curricular integration and research opportunities. One area that is not highlighted but warrants further exploration is the applicable lessons learned and models of service learning pedagogy. Discussion on education for sustainability is not novel. However, what is unique is the opportunity to fuse existing innovative pedagogical models in a manner that responds to the desired learning outcomes related to sustainability. The purpose of this article is to explore how an existing pedagogical model known as *service learning* could be harnessed and expanded as a heuristic model by which to educate and engage students with respect to the complex nature of sustainability.

The Heuristic Role of Sustainability

The notion of sustainability is portrayed in contemporary papers as the interaction between environmental resources and economic development (Froger and Zyla, 1998). Additionally, the success of sustainability as a concept lies in its ability to play a heuristic role that brings together the apparent necessity for economic growth, the need to preserve the environment, and the role of cultural integrity (Froger and Zyla, 1998). Rees (2003), author of *Our Ecological Footprint* writes, "There is little question that the world is on an unsustainable development path. There is even a consensus among scientists in various fields that excess energy and material consumption is at the heart of the problem. Critical resource systems are being overtaxed and global waste sinks filled to overflowing" (p. 89).

Environmental disruptions continue to manifest themselves in the form of water contamination, desertification, air pollution, loss of farmland, and depleted fisheries. Natural resources are no longer abundant; the temperature of the earth is increasing, threatening us with the risks of global climate change; and plant and animal species are becoming extinct (Brown, 2001). Despite access to the continuous research that has led to detailed knowledge of the complex ecological interdependencies and indicators of environmental degradation, society continues to act in ways that have a devastating impact on the ecological community and human health (Chechile, 1991). This is the narrative that lays the foundation for the challenge of sustainability and begs the question as to what educational models can be expanded with the intent to expose students to these pressing issues.

Service Learning as a Pedagogical Framework

University students have a tendency to seek knowledge and skills more affiliated with job acquisition and less on how to apply that knowledge to real-world issues outside the classroom (Grossman, 2004). Concurrently, university coursework tends to be grounded in knowledge acquisition as achieved through literature and in-class discussion. Kezar and Rhoads (2001) argue that the recent growth in service learning may be a response to three general critiques of academia: lack of curricular relevance, lack of faculty commitment to teaching, and lack of institutional responsiveness to the larger public good. In response, a focus on sustainability would furnish curricular relevance, engage faculty in the project development process, and contribute to what Kezar and Rhoads (2001) refer to as the "larger public good."

Service learning, as applied to the educational context within colleges and universities, conjures up an image of linking some form of community service (charity or social justice based) to an academic area of study (by way of a class; Pearce, 2006). A comprehensive definition of service learning expands on this pedagogical approach:

> It is first and foremost a teaching methodology, more than a values model or a leadership development model or a social responsibility model. Second, there is an intentional effort made to utilize the community based learning on behalf of academic learning, and to utilize academic learning to inform community service. This presupposes that academic service learning will not happen unless concerted effort is made to harvest community based learning and strategically bridge it with academic learning. Third, there is an integration of the two kinds of learning—experiential and academic; they work to strengthen one another. And last, the community service experiences must be relevant to the academic course of study |Markus, Howard, and King, 1993, p. 411|.

Extracting from the theory, many universities have developed their own models of service learning with the intent of connecting the classroom to the community. One example of how this model has been adopted and mainstreamed by a university is the program at Middlebury College in Vermont. Middlebury promotes service learning as "a credit-bearing, educational experience in which students participate in an organized service activity that meets identified community needs and reflect on the service activity in such a way as to gain further understanding of course content, a broader appreciation of the discipline, and an enhanced sense of civic responsibility."

Middlebury College also makes it a point to illustrate what service learning is *not*, in an attempt to illustrate what it is. The explanation goes on to articulate that service learning cannot be interchanged with the terms *volunteerism, community service, internship,* or *field education.* Beyond the definition of what service learning ought to be, there remain a number of questions with respect to how service learning fits into the educational goals of a college or university. Kezar and Rhoads (2001) articulate and explore a number of these questions in their research with respect to desired learning outcomes:

• What are the desired learning outcomes linked to student development, including promotion of citizenship, social responsibility, and perhaps moral commitment?
• How do organizational structures affect the ability of service learning to meet educational goals?
• What key features ought to be included as part of constructing service-learning experiences?

Prior to embarking on the task of developing a service learning model for sustainability, the educator must articulate the desired learning outcomes as well as the desired social outcomes within the institution. This approach warrants recognition of the embedded complexity of the organizational systems with which the service learning projects would engage.

From Service to Learning for Sustainability

For the purpose of this discussion, I draw from and build on the work of the theorists Lewis (2004) and Marullo and Edwards (2000). They distinguish between two prevalent models of service learning: social justice and charity. The social justice model tends to frame the educational opportunity in the context of community empowerment and the creation of more equitable institutional structures. The charity model tends to focus the educational experience and exchange on serving less privileged individuals and communities (Marullo and Edwards, 2000).

Grounded in the lessons learned from the work of Lewis and Marullo and Edwards, with respect to the discussion on how universities can advance the objectives of sustainable development I offer a model of service learning for sustainability. The model must be developed in the context of how a university is able to integrate and advance the respective principles and goals of sustainable development. The proposed service learning for sustainability model is framed by Lewis's five categories, which apply the lessons learned from these two existing models (see Table 2.1).

If a service learning model is adopted as a pedagogical framework for teaching about sustainability, the campus can be used as the source for the projects. Using the "campus as the classroom" is not a new concept (Orr, 1992). However, what distinguishes the proposed sustainability model from the social justice and charity model are the distinct characteristics as categorized originally by Lewis (2004; see Table 2.1). The contacts on campus

Table 2.1. Developing a Model of Service Learning for Sustainability

	Charity Model	Social Justice Model	Sustainability
Contacts	Agency-Based	Community-Based	Campus-Based
View of community	Community as subject	Community as partner	Campus as subject and partner
Objectives	Student learning plus service	Community empowerment plus student learning	Student learning plus campus as classroom
View of society	Consensus model: reform	Conflict model: transformation	Integrative model: critical analysis
Parallels in community-based research	Action research	Participatory, action research	Participatory, action research

Note: Supporting source, Lewis (2004).

range from the engineers, chefs, custodial managers, and grounds workers to the procurement officers, administrators, and faculty. This model requires a working set of relationships between faculty and operational staff. Moreover, it shifts the academic tendency to value off-site models as having rigor and value to onsite. If the campus is embraced as a learning tool, then the view of community shifts from looking outside the walls of the university to valuing campus operations and organizational structure as a teaching tool. Framed by Lewis's view of society (2004), sustainability education requires both the educator and the learner to assume an integrative approach that calls for a multidisciplinary framework for thinking, learning, and critical analysis. Ultimately, the desired educational outcomes would be for the students to comprehend what it means to live within the limits of the earth's natural systems and how this applies to the decisions made on a university campus. Lastly, as called on by a community-based research approach, students would be required to engage in participatory, action-based research within the campus systems.

The commitment to becoming a sustainable campus is a transformative and long-term process. The campus is a unique and dynamic learning environment that constitutes a microcosm of the larger community. Many of the issues discussed in the classrooms of courses taught in departments such as engineering, environmental studies, public health, business, and architecture can be found within the organizational structure of the institution. The educational opportunities will fluctuate from year to year as the campus takes on a variety of issues: greenhouse reduction strategies, energy conservation, the role of biofuels, green cleaning strategies, local food in the dining hall, overall community engagement. Opportunities for development of potential service to learning projects are illustrated in Table 2.2.

Table 2.2. Sustainable Systems Interface for Service Learning

Operational system	Client	Goal	Task
Transportation	Parking and Transit Department	Reduce single occupancy vehicles on campus	Analysis of commuter preference and response to alternatives
Energy	Systems Engineering	Decrease greenhouse gas emissions	Conduct a greenhouse gas inventory
Maintenance	Custodial Services	Use less harmful products for cleaning	Do comparative analysis of new green products on the market
Waste management	Custodial Services and Recycling	Reduce, reuse, recycle	Assess student waste production habits
Land and management	Grounds Mainte-nance; Environmental Healt hand Safety	Apply nonharmful products to landscape	Conduct a tree inventory
Food services	Dining Services	Incorporate local and organic food into campus dining	Analyze food miles traveled for specific menu items; link to greenhouse gas emissions

Development of a service learning for sustainability model, based on the social justice and charity framework, forces the educator to shift the pedagogical construction from needing to offer service for a less privileged person or agency outside of the walls of the university to valuing campus departments as viable agencies with whom to engage in a service to learning relationship. I would argue that it is the overarching context of a university commitment to becoming a sustainable campus that enables this pedagogical evolution. Table 2.2 illustrates the potential operational areas on a campus with which a client-class relationship could be developed along with a list of sample goals and tasks. As universities set out to develop sustainable operational systems, new knowledge and analytical skills are needed and a new set of questions emerges. If successful, the operational functions as outlined in Table 2.2 will be recognized in the context of a dynamic and complex campus system that provides educational value.

Conclusion

In summary I would like to outline four thoughts for consideration. First, acknowledging the campus as a classroom and client must be an intentional choice on the part of the institution. A commitment to developing a *service learning for sustainability* model on campus calls for setting in motion the

NEW DIRECTIONS FOR HIGHER EDUCATION • DOI: 10.1002/he

relationships needed with the various campus departments. As Kezar and Rhoads (2001) suggested, there are a number of questions that have to be considered before implementing this model. For example, "How do organizational structures impact the ability of service learning to meet educational goals?" (p. 149) Second, a set of desired learning and social outcomes with respect to sustainability must be outlined. Again, Kezar and Rhoads pose the relevant question: "What key features ought to be included as part of constructing service-learning experiences?" (p. 149). Third, a system to present the final products from the service learning projects must be established prior to implementation. The primary objective is to ensure that these projects do not merely remain an intellectual exercise and framed as research but rather contribute to the sustainability momentum of the campus. Moreover, those who oversee the operational functions of an institution tend to be quite removed from academic systems. If successful, the projects could lead to ongoing relationships between faculty and operational staff. Fourth, "community needs" as previously defined by the charity and social model ought to be redefined in the context of campus sustainability. This will lead to reconceptualization of our view of what community is and the benefits that can be secured by this service and the interdepartmental relationships that ensue.

References

Brown, L., Flavin, C., and French, H. *State of the World, 2001*. New York: Norton, 2001.
Chechile, R. A. "Introduction to Environmental Decision-Making." In R. A. Chechile and S. Carlisle (eds.), *Environmental Decision Making: A Multidisciplinary Perspective.* New York: Van Nostrand Reinhold, 1991.
Froger, G., and Zyla, E. "Towards a Decision-Making Framework to Address Sustainable Development Issues." In S. Faucheux, M. O'Connor, and J. van der Straaten (eds.), Sustainable Development: Concepts, Rationalities and Strategies. Dordrecht, Netherlands: Kluwer Academic, 1998.
Grossman, J. "Linking Environmental Science Students to External Community Partners: A Critical Assessment of a Service Learning Course." *Journal of College Science Teaching,* 2004, *33*(5), 32–35.
Kezar, A., and Rhoads, R. "The Dynamic Tensions of Service Learning in Higher Education: A Philosophical Perspective." *Journal of Higher Education,* 2001, *72*(2), 148–171.
Lewis, T. L. "Service Learning for Social Change? Lessons from a Liberal Arts College." *Teaching Sociology,* 2004, *32*(1), 94–108.
Markus, G., Howard, J., and King, D. "Integrating Community Service and Classroom Instruction Enhances Learning: Results from an Experiment." *Educational Evaluation and Policy Analysis,* 1993, *15*(4), 410–419.
Marullo, S., and Edwards, B. "From Charity to Justice: The Potential of University-Community Collaboration for Social Change." American Behavioral Scientist, 2000, 43, 895–899.
McIntosh, M., Cacciola, K., Clermont, S., Keniry, J. *State of the Campus Environment: A National Report Card on Environmental Performance and Sustainability in Higher Education.* Reston, Va: National Wildlife Federation, 2001.
Orr, D. *Ecological Literacy*. Albany: State University of New York Press, 1992.
Orr, D. *Earth in Mind: On Education, Environment, and the Human Prospect*. Washington, D.C.: Island Press, 1994.

Pearce, J. "Service Learning in Engineering and Science for Sustainable Development." *International Journal for Service Learning in Engineering,* 2006, 1(1), 1–4.

Rees, W. *Our Ecological Footprint: Reducing Human Impact on the Earth.* Gabriola Island, B.C., Canada: New Society, 1996.

JULIE NEWMAN is the director and founder of the Yale University Office of Sustainability.

3

Colleges cannot avoid teaching ethics across their undergraduate curriculums, but they can be deliberate in approach rather than uncoordinated.

Ethics Across the Curriculum

Nancy J. Matchett

All colleges teach ethics across their undergraduate curricula, yet relatively few institutions do so deliberately. That is, few colleges make explicit attempts to coordinate or integrate the various ethical lessons their students might be learning. This does not mean that most colleges are bad for students' ethical development; research shows that total years of formal education is a far more powerful predictor of moral judgment development than any other variable (McNeel, 1994; Nucci and Pascarella, 1987; Rest, 1994), and most of the knowledge and skills that students acquire during their undergraduate years are undoubtedly good for their character in some broad sense. Still, the failure to devote sustained attention to precisely *what* ethical messages students are receiving and to *how* those messages are being conveyed has a number of unintended consequences, at least some of which are worrisome from an ethical point of view.

In addition to highlighting the potentially worrisome features of an uncoordinated approach, this chapter identifies a basic set of ethics learning outcomes that can be intentionally pursued without (1) threatening the academic freedom of individual faculty members or (2) suggesting that all campuses should adopt a monolithic, one-size-fits-all model. This is possible, because the most important ethical outcomes are "deliberative" in character; that is, they have more to do with cultivating students' capacity to deliberate meaningfully and responsibly about ethics than with teaching a single decision procedure or recommending a particular set of values, principles, or norms. (Of course, deliberative outcomes are also compatible with more specific recommendations of this sort.) These same deliberative outcomes can be used to offer professional development opportunities to faculty and staff (Boylan and Donahue, 2003; Davis, 2004; Ozar, 2001), and even to

NEW DIRECTIONS FOR HIGHER EDUCATION, no. 142, Summer 2008 © Wiley Periodicals, Inc.
Published online in Wiley InterScience (www.interscience.wiley.com) • DOI: 10.1002/he.301

ensure that the decisions made by campus administrators model the deliberative approach to ethics that the undergraduate curriculum is designed to
facilitate (Boylan and Donahue, 2003). Hence, institutions can use this
approach to develop "ethics across the curriculum" (EAC) programs that
truly integrate the entire campus community.

Current Approaches to Ethics Across the Curriculum

Michael Davis (2004) has pointed out that there are at least five things the
phrase "ethics across the curriculum" might mean. Larry Hinman (1999)
has suggested that EAC programs be conceived as falling somewhere within
two overlapping spectrums: they may be more or less centralized (ranging
from those that require at least one course taught by a specialist in philosophical ethics to those that offer ethics units in an array of courses taught
by faculty with no formal training in ethical theory or practice), or they may
be more or less academic (from those that require coursework in ethics to
those that require some sort of community service or volunteer activity).
Even those programs that are consciously designed to fall somewhere within
Hinman's schema typically coordinate EAC activities within a fairly limited
sphere, and the majority of institutions do not have coordinated EAC programs at all. A few require students to take at least one course in "ethics" or
"values" or "contemporary issues." A few more have required courses in one
or more preprofessional majors designed to familiarize students with the relevant codes of ethics in those fields, and nearly all have at least some elec-
tive courses in which ethical topics are discussed. Many foster opportunities
for students to engage in campus leadership and community service, and
most have a mission and values statement calling attention to the "core values" all members of the community are expected to uphold. But only a
handful of institutions make explicit attempts to facilitate ongoing student
reflection about the relationship between the different "ethics" they might
be exposed to during their college years.[1] The majority of institutions offer
a host of courses in which neither the value commitments assumed by the
general course discipline nor any ethical issues related to the specific course
subject matter are ever explicitly discussed.

There are, of course, some good reasons for this. Lack of time is one of
them. There are many important things students might learn about the topic
of any course, and anyone who has written a syllabus knows that hard
choices about content must almost always be made. Lack of expertise is
another. Many nonethics faculty have fairly limited ideas about how they
might lead a productive discussion about ethical issues related to their
course subject matter, and they sensibly fear that attempts to do so will
devolve into a classroom shouting match. Nonethics faculty also tend to be
very unsure about the criteria they might use to fairly assess student ethical
thinking. These two pressures are often combined, with the result that
even those faculty who might like to explore ethical considerations that are

NEW DIRECTIONS FOR HIGHER EDUCATION • DOI: 10.1002/he

relevant to their courses ultimately conclude that, rather than treating them superficially, it is better to avoid them altogether. Because few administrators have reason to challenge faculty judgments on this score, many conclude that EAC programs cannot be deliberately implemented without threatening faculty control over their own classrooms.

There are also some not-so-good reasons for the lack of campuswide attention to ethics. Some faculty may simply not see or be interested in the connections between ethics and the courses they teach. Others may be uncomfortable with the thought that their job involves "inculcating values" or "building character" in their students, believing that the only legitimate role for higher education in a pluralistic society is to engage in forms of inquiry that are more purely academic or even value-free. Some may even be convinced that ethics has little to do with the intellectual life at all—that ethical judgments are really just expressions of personal taste, or that ethical behavior is the result of prior socialization and unreflective emotional response. Campuses where such thoughts are shared by the administration will not necessarily avoid EAC altogether, but if they do incorporate some kind of EAC program, it will typically fall exclusively within the domain of student and residential life.

At least four things can be said about why this second group of reasons is less convincing than the first. First, they largely ignore the fact that ethical questions are at the core of most disciplines (Simon, 2003). Second, they overlook the fact that nearly all courses raise ethical questions for students, despite an instructor's best efforts to cordon off those questions (McKeachie, 2002; Simon, 2003). Third, the picture of ethics as resting entirely on socialization ignores the overwhelming body of evidence that moral judgment is deeply related to cognition (Kohlberg, 1981, 1984; Rest, 1979, 1994). Fourth, the socialization model ultimately suggests that how ethical a person turns out to be is almost entirely a matter of luck. This is antidemocratic, and antithetical to nearly everything else that is said about the purpose of a college degree.

However, there is at least one way in which the socialization model of ethics presupposed by this second group is clearly correct. Students are constantly absorbing all sorts of implicit lessons about ethics, even on campuses without any sort of EAC program, and often in courses where faculty might think that no ethics teaching is being done. This includes the myriad lessons transmitted via nonacademic activities and students' daily interactions with their peers. Precisely because so many of these lessons are taught and learned unreflectively, they may be accepted as ethically obvious despite some rather serious flaws.

Unintentional Outcomes of an Uncoordinated Approach

One of these unfortunate lessons is the view that ethics is completely relative or even subjective, and hence that cultural practices or personal feelings "constitute the ultimate criterion of right and wrong" (Ashmore, 1991, p. 16).

NEW DIRECTIONS FOR HIGHER EDUCATION • DOI: 10.1002/he

As Steven Satris has pointed out, the form of relativism embraced by college students is more often used as an "invincible suit of armor" to "prevent or close off dialog and thought" than held as a well-thought-out position on the nature of ethics itself (Satris, 1986, p. 198). Still, the uncritical acceptance of relativism and the superficial forms of tolerance that go with it are supported by numerous college experiences.

Most obviously, undergraduates are immediately confronted by conflict between their own ethical values and the values of their peers. Much of their coursework will confirm the fact that people's ethical outlooks are often the product of social forces over which they have fairly limited control. Though this is especially true in the social sciences, where the primary goal often just *is* to illuminate precisely how these social forces work, the notion that ethics itself (as opposed to specific *beliefs* about ethics) is inherently relative is also conveyed whenever a student "discovers" that ethics means one thing in Professor Smith's class but something different in Professor Jones's. Of course, there are perfectly legitimate reasons Smith and Jones might be teaching subtly different "ethics." Perhaps Smith is a proponent of Classical Utilitarianism, while Jones has been persuaded by the theories of Aristotle or Kant. Or perhaps Smith teaches courses in business focused on the organizational requirements for ethics compliance, while Jones teaches courses in literature where questions of character and moral identity come to the fore. It is doubtful that Professors Smith and Jones intend for their students to get the message that ethics is completely relative, just as it is doubtful that social scientists intend for their students to learn that the mere fact something is believed by a culture is enough to prove it is socially useful, let alone that it might be true. But unless they are offered repeated opportunities to reflect on the deep incoherence of relativistic points of view (is the claim "all ethical values are relative" true for *everyone,* or only those people who happen to believe the claim already?) and the reasons such viewpoints do *not* suggest that people ought to be tolerant (in fact, they imply that individuals or cultures who sincerely believe they are ethically bound to impose their values on others are completely justified in doing so), students are unlikely to do the hard work involved in constructing a more substantive ethical worldview (Satris, 1986; Boylan and Donahue, 2003).

Another closely related but equally unfortunate lesson is that ethics necessarily involves obedience to some external authority. Culture might be thought to serve as an authority in this sense, but so might the government, or a god, or any other institution or person who holds a position of social power. This lesson too is conveyed in numerous ways—most obviously, by the fact that most campuses have an ethics code. Because students face an array of penalties for violating the campus code, they have little motivation to question it, and on most campuses students are rarely offered serious opportunities to explore why their campus code contains the specific content that it does. Students may learn about ethics codes in some of their other courses too, and in such courses codes are typically presented as a list of values and principles that one *must* embrace to be a member of a particular profession. Aspiring professional students again have little motivation to critically examine the content of such codes on their own, and in part because of the pressures of time and expertise mentioned earlier neither do students typically have the opportunity to explore their deeper meaning and justification, let alone the relationship of such codes to the students' more private or personal ethical views. This, or course, feeds back into their uncritical relativism; it begins to look as though ethics must mean one thing in public or professional life, quite another in the private sphere.

It is not only in preprofessional courses that lessons about authoritative ethics are unwittingly being "taught." As Michael Boylan and James Donahue point out, "Values enter into what we study, how we study it, and what we do with the results once they are published" (2003, pp. 23–24). Because nearly every discipline assumes or even requires certain ethical commitments, the majority of "so called value-free teaching is simply advocacy by default" (McKeachie, 2002, p. 292). [2] That this is the case becomes immediately evident when we imagine the sort of response a student might get on expressing ethical worries about the material in any given course. "Well, in order to learn some very important facts we have to engage in this sort of inquiry," a professor might say. Or "That's an interesting criticism, but everyone in this field begins from the assumption that this is appropriate. You can't understand the important insights in this reading material unless you go along with that assumption, at least for now."

The point here is neither that professors want their students to blindly accept certain ethical teachings nor that ethics codes and disciplinary value commitments lack any deeper justification. Rather, the point is that we should be wary of the cumulative effect of repeated exposure to these seemingly authoritative ethics. Steven McNeel (1994) has found that programs tending to close off ethical questioning and ethical inquiry inhibit growth in moral judgment. As Stanley Milgram's famous experiments in the 1960s made clear, it is far too easy for even well-educated people to uncritically accept the commands of legitimate social authorities. Unless students are given repeated opportunities to develop the critical reasoning and reflective skills that would enable them to articulate why (or whether) a particular activity is indeed ethical (or unethical), independently of some authoritative structure, there is at least some reason to worry about the effects of college on their sense of personal integrity.

This is related to a third unfortunate lesson of an uncoordinated approach: that ethical deliberation is in some sense less important or serious than other forms of scholarly inquiry, that it has little to do with fact checking and rigorous analysis, or that it is a special kind of inquiry frequently distracting a person's attention from more "tangible" or "objective" concerns. This lesson is perhaps most likely to be conveyed on campuses where most of the officially sanctioned EAC activities fall under the purview of student and residential life, but it is not taught solely by those who advocate the "ethics-as-socialization" view described earlier. Ironically, it too is often conveyed by precisely those faculty who avoid explicit discussion of ethical topics out of concern that they lack the time and expertise to give them the attention they are due. "That's an excellent and important question," such a professor might say in response to a student question. "But unfortunately it's not one that professors in my field are trained to deal with. If you're really interested in questions like that, you should try a course in philosophy or religious studies." Or, "Yep, that's an issue. But it's one of those things we could end up talking about all day without being able to reach any conclusion. So let's just bracket it off to make sure we have time to finish up with our main topic." To be sure, such comments do not quite *say* that ethical questions cannot be pursued through reasoned inquiry, and this is almost certainly not the lesson that professors who say these things want their students to learn. Still, when combined with the so-called lessons about relativism and authority that are swirling about in the air surrounding undergraduates, this may be precisely what students hear.

The Need for a Deliberative Approach

Attempts to establish highly coordinated EAC programs often bog down in debate about *whose values* will be taught. But because we have seen that it is impossible for colleges to avoid teaching values, this cannot be the most pressing issue. If anything, the average college student probably should have more values, not fewer, so there is at least a *prima facie* reason for teaching them all. Though frequent exposure to potentially conflicting values can lead to the uncritical relativism and obedience to authority that a good EAC program should seek to avoid, this probably has less to do with the content of the values to which students may be exposed than with the *way* in which lessons about values are taught. It is unlikely that college students require protection from values with controversial content (and even if they did, it is extremely unlikely that institutions could supply such protection). What they should possess are the deliberative skills that enable them to determine *which* of the values they are exposed to—during college, and throughout their adult lives—are worthy of their allegiance, to notice *when* they are in a situation where issues of value are especially significant, and to figure out *what* they should do when confronted by a situation where values inevitably conflict.[3] Hence, cultivating ethical deliberation should be the central focus of EAC.

Although ethical deliberation is a necessarily open-ended process, it can be usefully characterized by three main features. First, it goes beyond simply following a code or system of rules, even when those rules are uncontroversial. Even though rules such as "be kind," "tell the truth," and "promote the general good" might help us be more ethical, we have to notice when we are in a situation to which the rules apply if they are to be of any real use. Because every person faces slightly differing circumstances, we also have to understand how the rules can be applied to a variety of situations. Similarly, there are times when we want to figure out which rules are justified, how they should be prioritized, or whether any of the usual rules are even applicable. The fact that judgments of this sort often depend crucially on the details of the particular case is one reason frequently given in favor of EAC programs: understanding those details thoroughly requires input from numerous disciplines (Hinman, 1999; Simon, 2003; Ozar, 2001). Still, the ethical significance of those details cannot be understood without developing deliberative skills that enable us to (1) identify relevant values, principles, or ideals and (2) meaningfully connect them with the relevant facts.

Second, ethical deliberation is an ongoing activity that lies in the background of all human endeavors. It is not a special kind of thinking, or something that we can decide to engage in now and then. This is because every choice has an ethical dimension; every choice reveals something about what we currently value, and in a broader sense what kind of people we really are. Put another way, ethical deliberation is inherently practical. Its point is never simply to figure out what we should think or believe (though that is an important part of the process); rather, its point is to figure out *what we should do*. Because even the skeptical question "Why should we bother about ethics?" is a question about why we should live our lives according to some values or principles rather than others, ethical deliberation turns out to be inescapable for anyone who values anything at all.

Katherine Simon has emphasized that students are constantly asking this kind of question about their classwork (Simon, 2003). Teachers may be fascinated by the purely intellectual intricacies of their field, but students are constantly trying to figure out how the things they study *matter* to their daily lives. Hence, in addition to helping students develop ethical deliberation skills, EAC programs are likely to increase student interest in their coursework. In fact, students consistently report very a high level of satisfaction in courses that incorporate ethical reflection (Davis, 2006).

This explains why ethics is so often deeply personal (and why the temptation to use relativism as a protective "suit of armor" is ever-present). But the third feature of ethical deliberation is that it is never purely personal. Although each of us must ultimately be able to live with ourselves, we must also be able to live with other people. If we cannot justify our choices to anyone other than ourselves, we have at least some reason to question the adequacy of our own deliberations. Even if the best we can do sometimes is agree to disagree, ethics at least requires us to give some explanation of our conduct. This aspect of ethical deliberation connects with two additional justifications of EAC: repeated reflection on ethical issues in the classroom probably encourages continued reflection by students in the future, and professors serve as important role models when they demonstrate how ethical deliberation both shapes and informs their own professional lives (Hinman, 1999; Boylan and Donahue, 2003).

The foregoing suggests that the question for colleges is not whether to engage in EAC, but how to do it well. It also suggests that to do EAC well, institutions should focus on cultivating students' capacity for ethical deliberation. The most effective way to do this is to identify concrete learning outcomes toward which both teachers and learners might aim. Such an approach is beneficial to students; it helps them get clearer about what they are supposed to be learning in the area of ethical deliberation, as well as about how their various colleges experiences (academic and nonacademic) might be contributing to that learning. Such an approach is also beneficial to faculty and student programming staff—especially those who have little or no background in the area of ethics—because it helps them get clearer about how their specific subject matter, program content, or delivery methods might contribute to students' capacity for ethical deliberation more generally. An outcomes-centered approach is beneficial to institutions as a whole, because it enables the teaching and learning of ethical deliberation to be coordinated across a variety of college activities.

Teaching and Learning Outcomes for Ethical Deliberation

David Ozar has made substantial progress in specifying "Ideal Learning Outcomes for Undergraduate Ethics" (2001, the title of his Section Two). Following James Rest (1986), he notes that there are at least four important areas in which colleges can produce growth in ethical development. The first is "awareness or sensitivity to what is morally/ethically at stake" in a given situation (Ozar, 2001, p. 7). In this area, it is important for students to achieve[4]:

1. Knowledge of
   A. A wide array of values, principles, and ideals, including those that are especially relevant to specific professional roles the student might be training for
   B. Potential conflicts between those values, principles, and ideals
   C. Facts that are especially relevant to ethical decisions in specific areas (for example, legal facts about what is required of members in specific professions, or social scientific facts about the correlations between various sorts of incentives and punishments and various forms of human behavior)

as well as

2. Skills in
   A. Multiple perspective taking (the ability to understand or empathize with a variety of points of view)

Ozar's second area involves "reasoning and other reflective skills leading to judgments about what ought to be done" (2001, p. 7). These skills include:

B. Formulating arguments that are logical (conclusions are supported by reasons), careful (the argument does not rely on hidden assumptions or mask important objections), and clear (key concepts are defined explicitly and used consistently)
C. Employing "useful conceptual tools" (for example, well-established ethical theories)
D. Accurately applying standards that are commonly expected in both ordinary and professional social roles (for example, the principles and virtues embodied by specific ethics codes)

It is important to note that the knowledge and skills across these two areas are deeply intertwined. Most obviously, skill in employing typical standards (item 2.D.) requires knowledge of what those standards are (item 1.A.). Similarly, knowledge of an array of values (item 1.A.) will likely enhance the ability to take multiple perspectives (item 2.A.), just as skill in multiple perspective taking will typically lead to an expanded knowledge of values.

Once we recognize this, it is immediately obvious that the ability to employ "useful conceptual tools" (item 2.C.) surely requires knowledge about what those tools might be, and so it might seem that providing a more concrete specification of such tools is crucial to the task of identifying learning outcomes for ethical deliberation. However, there are both practical and philosophical reasons this is difficult to do with precision, especially in the abstract. The practical problem is that even a fairly cursory study of the history of ethical thought reveals a plethora of useful conceptual tools. These tools form the special area of expertise known as moral philosophy (also called philosophical ethics), and it is surely unreasonable to expect faculty and students from across the curriculum to become well versed in them all. The philosophical problem is that the specific tools we use to conceptualize ethical issues inevitably shape both our awareness of situations and the patterns of reasoning that we might use to support specific conclusions. EAC programs that specify the "useful conceptual tools" too narrowly run the risk of closing off legitimate avenues of ethical thought. But of course, the refusal to give or emphasize any specific set of conceptual tools makes it significantly less likely that progress in the area of "reasoning and reflective skills" can be achieved.

Specifically, students will be unable to integrate the learning done in one class or program with the learning done in another, and faculty (especially those who themselves lack knowledge of potentially useful tools for conceptualizing ethical issues that arise in their courses and disciplines) will be unable to coordinate their own teaching with the teaching done by their colleagues in other fields. Hence, although the situation with respect to

NEW DIRECTIONS FOR HIGHER EDUCATION • DOI: 10.1002/he

useful conceptual tools is similar to the situation with respect to values mentioned earlier, and there is again at least *a prima facie* reason for teaching as many as possible, it does seem fairly important for colleges to identify a core set of "conceptual tools" that can be used as a reference point for all EAC activities that take place on their campus. Committing to such a core facilitates a deeper understanding of how any of the tools that are employed (implicitly or explicitly) in specific courses and programs relate to all the others that may have been encountered (or may be encountered in the future), as well as how each tool contributes to the ongoing process of ethical deliberation. Hence, it makes it significantly more likely that students will be able to integrate those tools into a "personal ethical worldview" that avoids the uncritical forms of relativism, subjectivism, and authoritarianism discussed earlier (Boylan and Donahue, 2003). Still, because there is room for substantial variation with respect to precisely *which* and *how many* conceptual tools any particular campus should embrace, it is sufficient for our purposes here to add that EAC programs should pursue knowledge of some core set of conceptual tools. The mission and unique culture of any individual campus will determine the most appropriate tools.

Ozar's third and fourth areas of ethics teaching and learning are:

3. Motivation and conviction; that is, the conscious affirmation of and pattern of living habitually . . . in accord with [one's] moral or ethical judgments
4. Implementation; that is, the practical and emotional ability to carry out the course of action that [one] has judged ought to be done and is motivated to do [2001, p. 7]

Ozar himself does not attempt to specify more concrete learning outcomes in these areas, for a number of reasons. To begin with, student achievement in these areas is significantly more difficult to assess; motivation and implementation skills are revealed in ongoing patterns of behavior that extend well beyond the confines of any class assignment or program activity. Ozar hastens to add: the fact that certain outcomes may be more difficult to assess "does not make them less significant" (2001, p. 5); the point is only that it makes them more difficult to describe with precision.[5] In addition, "the commitment to open inquiry that is characteristic of higher education places severe limits on the ways in which faculty may promote or foster particular sets of motivations" (2001, p. 13), and the need to develop specific implementation skills is limited primarily to preprofessional roles. Hence for most campuses, growth in these two areas will necessarily be given a lower priority than growth in awareness and reasoning or reflection.

Even so, it is worth noting that knowledge and skills in all four of these areas are deeply intertwined. All ethical theories incorporate answers to the questions "Why be moral?" and "What is the best way of ensuring that all of us human beings do what we ought?" So here again, any choices about the most useful conceptual tools will inevitably highlight certain kinds of answers to these questions and not others. Because the point of ethical deliberation is to figure out what we should do, facilitating student abilities in the areas of motivation and implementation is crucial to their ethical growth. Hence there is no reason for individual faculty and staff to avoid pursuing specific outcomes in these areas, and there is no reason for institutions to avoid specifying more concrete outcomes in the areas of motivation and implementation on campuses where there is reason to think that such outcomes can be meaningfully pursued. But here again, there is every reason to attempt to relate teaching and learning in those areas with the conceptual tools that form the core of the campus's EAC program; doing so will enrich students' capacity for, and perhaps even deepen their general commitment to, the open-ended process of ethical deliberation that EAC programs should be designed to achieve.

In summary, learning outcomes for ethical deliberation should include:

1. Knowledge of
   A. An array of values, principles, and ideals
   B. Potential conflicts among those values, principles, and ideals
   C. Facts that are especially relevant to ethical decisions in specific areas
   D. A core set of "useful conceptual tools" (including the reasons the campus EAC program recommends those particular tools)
2. Skills in
   A. Multiple perspective taking
   B. Formulating arguments that are logical, careful, and clear
   C. Employing the tools identified in 1.D.
   D. Applying standards that are commonly expected in both ordinary and professional social roles
   E. Analyzing, evaluating, or otherwise relating any number of other tools and standards to those identified in 2.C. and 2.D.

Pursuing these outcomes deliberately can help campuses to avoid the negative consequences of an uncoordinated approach. Moreover, they can be implemented in a way that does not threaten faculty control over their own classrooms and that alleviates the perennial difficulties of lack of time and expertise.

Strategies for Implementation

Three things are necessary for an EAC program based on these deliberative outcomes to succeed. First, information about the conceptual tools that form the core of the program must be made available to all students early and often (Penn [1990] has demonstrated the usefulness of teaching basic ethical concepts directly). One way to do this is to make a formal course in ethics—one designed to develop both knowledge of useful conceptual tools and skill in employing them to a fairly wide range of contexts—a requirement for every student, ideally within the first semester or at the least within the first year. But this is unlikely to be feasible on most college campuses, because the number of faculty who are trained to teach such a course is too small (Ozar, 2001; Davis, 2004). Another possibility is to develop orientation week programming that introduces students to these conceptual tools, perhaps by demonstrating how they are relevant to thinking about both the content and the application of the campus's student conduct code (this has the additional advantage of familiarizing students with the code without simply presenting it as yet another "authoritative" ethic). Still another option in this area is to develop a Website that includes basic information about the core set of ethical concepts along with interactive features designed to help students apply those conceptual tools in a variety of contexts (for an example of such a site, see the Center for Ethical Deliberation, at www.mcb.unco.edu/ced). Of course, these three possibilities might also be used in combination. However, none of these options is sufficient on its own; unless students are given repeated opportunities to use this knowledge and these skills, they are unlikely to be well integrated in students' ethical self-understanding (Boylan and Donahue, 2003).

To ensure that students are exposed to useful conceptual tools *often* requires widespread campus buy-in to the EAC program itself. This does not mean that all faculty and programming staff must be compelled to teach all, or even any, of the core conceptual tools directly (though in some classes it will be perfectly natural and appropriate to do so); nor will it require most faculty to make major changes in their course content (though it may lead some faculty members to think about their own content decisions a bit differently). At most it requires subtle changes in how existing content is delivered—for example, being explicit about any ethical knowledge and skills assumed by their course content, and how they are related to EAC learning goals in general.

Similarly, nothing in the foregoing analysis suggests that individual faculty and programming staff should not go beyond a campus's core set of conceptual tools whenever their own expertise enables them to do so. At most, it suggests that if and when they go further, they use teaching strategies designed to help students see how their additional concepts relate to and supplement the more limited core. The important point is that faculty and staff will be able to do this more effectively if their reasoning is linked to conceptual tools with which their students are already familiar—that is, if their reasoning is explicitly linked to the EAC program's set of core conceptual tools.

This brings us to the second necessary element of a deliberate EAC program: widespread availability of workshops for both faculty and student programming staff. Such workshops serve the dual purpose of (1) making all campus constituencies aware of the campuswide EAC learning goals and (2) facilitating professional development of nonethics faculty and staff who would like to incorporate more ethics into their own classrooms and programs but are unsure how to go about doing so. As numerous commentators have pointed out, such workshops should carry a generous stipend if at all possible, because in addition to encouraging widespread participation this sends the message that ethical deliberation is a rigorous scholarly activity that merits sustained attention and institutional support (Ashmore, 1991; Boylan and Donahue, 2003; Davis, 2006; Hinman, 1999).

The primary goal of a workshop series is to expand knowledge and skills with respect to some set of core conceptual tools, because these are the tools with which nonethics faculty are least likely to be familiar, and with which all faculty should be minimally familiar in order to give students repeated opportunities to develop skills in employing them. (Most college faculty are quite adept at taking multiple perspectives and formulating arguments that are logical, careful, and clear; similarly, most are quite familiar with the broad range of values and principles that are assumed by their discipline, as well as potential conflicts both among those values and between those values and others.) But even though the process of specifying the core content for these workshops must begin with a group of faculty or administrators whose scholarly expertise in the field of ethics enables them to form reasonable hypotheses about the most basic conceptual tools that are likely to be most useful to students and faculty on their campus, there is no reason it should end there. Indeed, there is every hope that as faculty become increasingly adept at ethical deliberation, they will participate in ongoing conversations about the potential limits of existing tools, and the possibilities for incorporating new and better ones in the future.

The third element of a successful EAC program is that the campus be prepared to back it up—"not only in initiatives for faculty and students . . . but also through a self-study of how the administration itself is committed to the same mission" (Boylan and Donahue, 2003, p. 143). Perhaps the most effective way to do this is to set up a series of community forums designed to identify policies and procedures that go against the EAC learning outcomes, and to give all campus constituencies the opportunity to apply the knowledge and skills embodied in those outcomes in the process of developing constructive solutions. This presents a concrete model of the deliberative approach to ethics that is being recommended to the campus community. It also serves as an important reminder that although ethical deliberation is an ongoing and open-ended process, it is a process that really does produce practical results.

Notes

1. One especially notable exception is Alverno College in Wisconsin, which includes "valuing in decision making" as one of the eight specific components of its integrated Ability-Based Curriculum. Students demonstrate progress toward these outcomes by creating a digital portfolio. See *http://depts.alverno.edu/saal/abilities.html#abilities*.

2. McKeachie (2002) notes that even mathematics courses often employ standards of "beauty" or "simplicity," in a way that students find difficult to grasp unless professors are explicit about how these values are relevant to their discipline.

3. For this reason, James Rest's widely used Defining Issues Test of moral judgment is designed to determine the conceptual tools subjects use to think about moral issues, rather than the specific values subjects embrace.

4. Note that several modifications have been made to Ozar's own presentation of outcomes with each area, though all of his specific suggestions have been retained.

5. It is a central tenet of all outcomes-based approaches to learning that describing how one would assess whether a certain outcome was achieved is an important way of determining whether one's specification of that outcome is sufficiently concrete.

References

Ashmore, R. B. "A Marquette Experiment in Interdisciplinary Pedagogy." In R. B. Ashmore and W. C. Starr (eds.), *Ethics Across the Curriculum: The Marquette Experience*. Milwaukee, Wis.: Marquette University Press, 1991.

Boylan, M., and Donahue, J. A. *Ethics Across the Curriculum: A Practice-Based Approach*. San Francisco: Lexington Books, 2003.

Davis, M. "Five Kinds of Ethics Across the Curriculum: An Introduction to Four Experiments with One Kind." *Teaching Ethics*, 2004, 4(2), 1–14.

Davis, M. "IIT's Workshops for Integrating Ethics into Technical Courses: Some Lessons Learned." *Teaching Ethics*, 2006, 6(2), 1–14.

Hinman, L. "Ethics Across the Curriculum." Originally presented to the American Philosophical Association, Central Division, May 8, 1999. Retrieved 02/01/2008 from http://ethics.sandiego.edu/eac/Presentations/CentralAPA/EAC2_files/frame.htm.

Kohlberg, L. *The Philosophy of Moral Development, Vol. 1*. San Francisco: Harper & Row, 1981.

Kohlberg, L. *The Psychology of Moral Development, Vol. 2*. San Francisco: Harper & Row, 1984.

McKeachie, W. J. "Teaching Values: Should We? Can We?" In W. J. McKeachie and M. Svinicki (eds.), *McKeachie's Teaching Tips: Strategies, Research, and Theory for College and University Teachers* (11th ed.). Boston and New York: Houghton Mifflin, 2002.

McNeel, S. P. "College Teaching and Student Moral Development." In J. R. Rest and D. Narvaez (eds.), *Moral Development in the Professions. Psychology and Applied Ethics*. Hillsdale, N.J.: Erlbaum, 1994.

Nucci, L., and Pascarella, E. "The Influence of College on Moral Development." In J. Smart (ed.), *Higher Education: Handbook of Theory and Research, Vol. 3*. New York: Agathon, 1987.

Ozar, D. T. "An Outcomes Centered Approach to Teaching Ethics." *Teaching Ethics*, 2001, 2(1), 1–29.

Penn, W. Y., Jr. "Teaching Ethics: A Direct Approach." *Journal of Moral Education*, 1990, 19(2), 124–138.

Rest, J. R. *Development in Judging Moral Issues*. Minneapolis: University of Minnesota Press, 1979.

Rest, J. R. *Moral Development: Advances in Research and Theory*. New York: Praeger, 1986.

Rest, J. R. "Background: Theory and Research." In J. R. Rest and D. Narvaez (eds.), *Moral Development in the Professions: Psychology and Applied Ethics*. Hillsdale, N.J.: Erlbaum, 1994.

Satris, S. "Student Relativism." *Teaching Philosophy*, 1986, 9(3), 193–200.

Simon, K. G. *Moral Questions in the Classroom: How to Get Kids to Think Deeply About Real Life and Their Schoolwork*. (2nd ed.) New Haven and London: Yale University Press, 2003.

NANCY J. MATCHETT *is assistant professor of philosophy and director of the Institute of Professional Ethics at the University of Northern Colorado.*

4

By looking across discipline-specific codes of ethics, we can identify similarities that translate into general principles and specific ethical teaching behaviors.

Learning from the Codes of the Academic Disciplines

William D. Woody

Ethical questions have long been the impetus for philosophical inquiry around the world. University teachers must wrestle with the challenging goal of incorporating millennia of ethics research from many cultures into the demanding environment of a college or university classroom. When ethical questions arise in the classroom, during advising or in other academic settings, university and college instructors may appeal to the ethical codes within their own discipline for guidance. The materials that follow briefly review teaching-related sections of the professional codes of conduct from five disparate fields of scholarship (history, physics, engineering, nursing, and psychology) and seek common themes that can guide university and college instructors in general approaches to ethical dilemmas as well as specific situations. Across fields, ethical teaching reaches beyond classrooms; ethical teachers reinforce these ideas by modeling appropriate behavior, and ethical teachers seek to extend ethical behaviors beyond their students and into society at large. The article closes with appeals for explicit graduate education in ethics and for instructors to recognize the larger ethical context in which they teach.

Discipline-specific ethics codes vary widely, and each code seeks to guide those involved in the variety of activities subsumed within the discipline. The disciplines chosen for this article reflect a range of theoretical scholarship, basic science, applied science, and physical and mental health care. Despite this extensive breadth of topical areas, the selected ethics codes share common ground, and each addresses appropriate education and training within a discipline. The materials briefly address differences in the approaches of the chosen ethics codes and then more thoroughly explore similarities, particularly those that translate into tangible classroom behaviors for university and college teachers.

NEW DIRECTIONS FOR HIGHER EDUCATION, no. 142, Summer 2008 © Wiley Periodicals, Inc.
Published online in Wiley InterScience (www.interscience.wiley.com) • DOI: 10.1002/he.302

A central tenet implicit in this work is to inspire readers to examine the ethics codes of their own discipline and derive appropriate teaching guidance, regardless of whether their discipline has been selected for discussion here. Discipline-specific ethics codes reflect the goals, work environments, and particular ethical concerns of practitioners and educators within each field. Specifically, in the humanities, the American Historical Association (AHA; 2007a) initiates its code with emphasis on the "complex process of *critical dialogue*" (¶5; text appearing in italics in this sentence appears in bold in original) in history, "the trust and respect of both one's peers and of the public at large" (¶6), and the importance of "honoring *the integrity of the historical record*" (¶7). Basic and applied physicists in the American Physical Society (APS; 2008a) must maintain "professional integrity in the formulation, conduct, and reporting of physics activities" (¶2), and receive explicit guidance on dissemination of research results, determination of authorship, and appropriate peer review. These guidelines also receive support from a set of APS policy statements related to treatment of subordinates (2008b) and the elimination of discrimination (2008c, 2008d, 2008e). In an applied field, engineers face the challenge of ethically and appropriately applying findings from disparate areas of the material, mechanical, electrical, and computer sciences to the solution of practical problems. The fundamental canons of the National Society of Professional Engineers (NSPE; 2007) start with requirements to "hold paramount the safety, health, and welfare of the public" (¶3) and then emphasize competence, objective analysis, truthfulness, and the importance of each engineer's responsibilities to his or her employer. To guide practitioners, the International Council of Nurses (ICN; 2006) centers their ethics code on nurses' "primary professional responsibility . . . to people requiring nursing care" (p. 2). The American Psychological Association [APA] faces the challenge of developing an ethics code for mental health care providers, basic and applied researchers, and educators.

Despite the many differences across these disparate fields of scholarship, the codes emphasize development of knowledge, training of practitioners or researchers, and appropriate treatment of students or trainees. Each code emphasizes the importance of honesty, integrity, and respect in all activities, and teachers hope that these values transcend their classrooms and their students to influence society as a whole. Beyond these hopes and the specific details of each code, university and college instructors require greater depth in any discussion of application of simple ethical principles to the complex and potentially confusing world of the higher education classroom. The materials that follow move beyond the differences briefly described here and address the common ground. These materials explore common themes in ethical teaching, present specific ethical behaviors for university and college teachers, and support these themes with references to the discipline-specific codes. These central themes include competence, fairness, informed consent, appropriate relationships, and confidentiality.

NEW DIRECTIONS FOR HIGHER EDUCATION • DOI: 10.1002/he

Beyond these central themes, the article closes with the importance of explicitly teaching ethical behavior and seeing the larger ethical context in which university teachers live and work.

Competence

The several fields discussed in this chapter define competence in many ways. Researchers and scholars across fields must use appropriate methods to conduct and report research (AHA, 2007a; APS, 2008a; APA, 2002). Engineers must work within their areas of expertise (NSPE, 2007). Health practitioners, like engineers, are expected to recuse themselves from situations outside their professional competence. For example, nurses remain current in their education of medical procedures (ICN, 2006), and they must use professional judgment "when accepting and delegating responsibility" for the health of a patient (p. 3). Psychologists who are counselors or clinicians must "provide services . . . in areas only within the boundaries of their competence, based on their training, education, supervised experience, consultation, study, or professional experience" (APA, 2002, p. 1063). Teachers within these fields benefit from these definitions of competence, but competence in practice or scholarship may not translate into competence in teaching.

For university instructors, competence centers on knowledge of class topics and thorough preparation for each class session. Knowledge of class topics is itself multifaceted; instructors should possess thorough, correct, precise, and up-to-date knowledge of the topics addressed in each day's class. Instructors in applied arenas may require professional experience to competently prepare students for future employment. Although these criteria for competence appear straightforward, a national survey found that more than 90 percent of 482 psychology instructors in higher education reported having difficulty meeting these standards (Tabachnick, Keith-Spiegel, and Pope, 1991). Of course, few if any academics can know all of the material within their discipline or even within their own subfield, but all instructors share the common burden of being competent in the methodologies, background knowledge, and content presented in their own classrooms. These standards may be rather lofty, but instructors should strive to attain or approach competence in the limited areas included in their courses. For the sake of their own students as well as the future clients, students, patients, and others that the students will affect, teachers should attempt to explicitly model classroom competence.

Many obstacles exist between instructors and any measure of achievement of competence in the classroom. Administrators, particularly those at small institutions with limited staff for a range of courses, may assign an instructor to classes that are outside of the instructor's areas of expertise. Although many practitioners face limits on what jobs they may accept (for example, engineers may accept assignments "only when qualified by education or experience"

[NSPE, 2007, ¶4]), instructors may not have the administrative freedom to choose only their preferred classes. Additionally, academic or other administrators may prioritize research, grant funding, service, practice, or other duties over day-to-day classroom performance, and instructors may find that tangible rewards remain limited. Also, despite these limitations competent teaching requires assigning graduate or undergraduate classroom assistants fairly to tasks that fit their level of knowledge, time, and reward; instructors should not excessively delegate teaching activities to those without primary responsibility for the class. As discussed in the final section of this article, teachers' obligations to students and to student assistants transcend academic reward structures.Instructors pose models of scholarly behavior for students, and teachers must demonstrate with actions as well as words that standards of scholarship are meaningful and critical for the success of each individual, the members of the class as a whole, and the field of study. Instructors who teach practitioners face additional responsibilities because their successes or failures perpetuate as these successes or failures pass to the clients, students, or patients of the learners they teach. One professor of educational psychology begins his courses in Educational Psychology for Teachers by explicitly telling his students that, in his words, "I don't care about you" (Steven Pulos, personal communication, January, 2007). At this declaration, students often—predictably and appropriately—express frustration and dismay. He then clarifies that he does indeed care about them and their success as students and as people, but he cares more about the thousands of elementary and secondary students they will eventually teach. The professor then explains the high standards he expects his future teachers to achieve for the sake of the children whose lives they will shape.

Competent Teaching

Competence extends past knowledge and competence in the teacher's own area of research or practice to encompass competent teaching. Teachers must use appropriate teaching methods for each class. Appropriate methodologies for teaching vary widely with the teaching context. Obviously, advanced graduate scholars require different approaches, preparation, and delivery from those of new undergraduates in an introductory survey course. Instructors must fit each course to department, college, university, local, state, national, and potentially international standards and requirements for the course in specific, the program in general, and the students' future careers and opportunities. More specifically, these course goals can involve explicitly meeting guidelines or requirements, preparation of students for success in later courses and employment, and development of the students as future critical thinkers, scholars, and, for many fields, practitioners.

Beyond other ideas in this section, concerns have been raised by academics and in the popular press regarding bias in academic instruction (e.g., AAUP, 2004; Gravois, 2007; Klein, 2004), and some states have considered legislative action to address perceptions of political bias in university classrooms (Simpson, 2005). Teaching is an inherently persuasive activity (see Friedrich and Douglass, 1998), and teachers must introduce balanced perspectives (particularly about controversial areas), openly identify their own biases, model the processes by which scholars evaluate competing ideas, and encourage students to seek independent conclusions. These requirements to avoid bias present more significant challenges to instructors of ideologically challenging courses or classes that encompass such topics as religion, human sexual relations, and the history of race relations in the United States (see, for example, AHA, 2007a; Hester and Paloutzian, 2006; Finken, 2006).

Fairness

Requirements of professional fairness exist in all of the ethics codes considered in this article. The ethics codes for these disciplines contain strong and explicit statements against bias or discrimination based on age, gender, race, political affiliation, or religion (AHA, 2007b; APA, 2002; APS, 2008c; National Society for Professional Engineers: Professional Engineers in Industry [NSPEPEI], 2006). Some, but not all, codes explicitly address sexual orientation, culture, national origin, socioeconomic status, and gender identity (APA, 2002; APS, 2008c). Other codes do not attempt to present an exhaustive list of potential biases but note that all scholars, researchers, and practitioners must follow applicable legal guidelines (AHA, 2007b; APA, 2002; NSPEPEI, 2006) or uphold general principles regarding "human rights and . . . the values, customs, and beliefs of all people" (ICN, 2006, p. 5). Some ethics codes offer direct guidance on field-specific questions. For example, the American Physical Society issued a specific statement against hostile environment sexual harassment of women (APS, 2008d), and nurses' guidelines emphasize "human rights, equity, justice, [and] solidarity as the basis for access to care" (ICN, 2006, p. 5).[1] Fairness and elimination of bias connect ethical statements across all fields.

The importance of fairness in teaching cannot be overstated. Fair treatment of students is a central component of fair access to education; these issues reach beyond classrooms to public and legislative goals. Students as well as teachers recognize that fairness is critical for maintaining the credibility of departments, universities, and scholarly fields in general (Keith-Spiegel, Tabachnick and Allen, 1993; Tabachnick, Keith-Spiegel, and Pope, 1991). Fairness encompasses many behaviors. Teachers must avoid any bias against or in favor of students[2] for any reason listed in the preceding paragraph or any other, such as a student's social, religious, or athletic affiliation or even the degree to which a teacher likes or dislikes a student. Teachers must investigate their own biases for and against students to carefully avoid conferring any advantage or disadvantage on a student for any reason. College and university teachers, however, are human, and many biases are difficult if not impossible to eliminate (see Andersen, Moskowitz, Blair, and Nosek, 2007), but instructors must strive to separate personal evaluations from academic evaluations. Some instructors reduce potential bias by supplying very specific guidelines for all student assignments (for example, even going so far as to dictate font style, font size, and margin size) and then randomly assigning each student a number so that students remain anonymous. With these safeguards, students cannot be identified by name, and potential bias from faculty becomes less likely to influence academic outcomes. As discussed previously regarding competence, teachers model nondiscriminatory behavior for their students, and teacher bias can have effects that reach far beyond the classroom, particularly, as noted above, for those who teach future practitioners.

Fairness extends beyond avoiding discrimination. Not all students speak English as a native language, and many native English speakers do not grow up in a home environment that embraces the grammatical requirements of academic English. Writing for academia may involve learning new ways to use language—a difficult prospect in adulthood. Additionally, students from some cultures may value speed less than quality; timed testing may be particularly hard for these students in ways that extend beyond the difficulty of the material (see Suinn, 2005). In addition to questions of language and culture, in 2004 an estimated 6.8 percent of incoming students at four-year institutions of higher education reported disabilities, and an increasing number of students report learning disabilities (Ward and Merves, 2006). Additionally, many students are not diagnosed with learning or other disabilities until they arrive at a college or university, and some of these students do not yet know the accommodations that will best fit them. Instructors must maintain fairness for students with and without disabilities, and a difficult balance exists between maintaining the rigor and integrity of an examination while making accommodations for the testing needs of a student with a learning disability. Too often, this balance appears elusive. Rigid and blind equal treatment of all students does not ensure a level playing field for student performance (Wittig and others, 1999). Van Note Chism (2001) notes that teachers have obligations, when possible, to fit course activities, requirements, and examinations to the individual student's unique needs. In this process, students may also learn more about the accommodations that are effective learning tools for them, and students can take this knowledge into the workforce and potentially share these methods with others. A student-centered approach allows the student to be the expert on his or her abilities, and the teacher—hopefully with the support of college or university resources for students with disabilities—can fairly and rigorously meet each student's needs.

Fairness in teaching activities extends beyond bias and beyond testing. To maintain fairness and prevent any student from gaining unfair advantage, instructors must take reasonable steps to prevent and punish cheating, plagiarism, and other forms of academic dishonesty (Cizek, 2006). Extra credit, if used in a class, must reflect class material and be equally available to all students (Palladino, Hill, and Norcross, 1999). For example, an electrical engineering instructor should not offer extra credit for voting in a presidential election, and extra credit should not require attendance at an off-campus evening function because not all students are physically able to drive and some have caregiving requirements that preclude such activities. In these or similar situations (for example, if an instructor offers extra credit for voluntary research participation within the same scholarly field as the class), there must be an alternative method of acquiring the extra credit (Palladino, Hill, and Norcross, 1999). In a similar vein, in attempting to replicate realistic job or practice situations many instructors turn to group projects, particularly in fields where future graduates are likely to work in teams. Any instructor who assigns a group project must monitor individual efforts so that each group member's grade is commensurate with his or her contributions to the project.

Fairness must be a priority in advising, mentoring, and other teaching situations outside of the classroom. Some ethics codes include determination of authorship order and credit as an area of potential ethical conflict (e.g., AHA, 2007a; APA, 2002). Particularly when conducting research with students, determination of authorship order should be discussed early in the project so that authorship reflects each individual's contributions to the published product; this idea is a new addition to the most recent APA code 92002, and its presence testifies to the need for inclusion in psychology as well as other fields (see Smith, 2003). Across all areas of teaching and learning, the instructor carries the responsibility to reward students' successes, failures, and efforts as equitably and fairly as possible.

Informed Consent

The ethics codes discussed in this article require informed consent as appropriate for each field, and these concerns extend to the obligations of teachers in these arenas. Historians have obligations to inform scholars and lay readers about any potential biases that they bring to their work, including "*financial support,* sponsorship, or unique privileges . . . especially when such privileges could bias their research findings" (AHA, 2007a, ¶20; emphasis is bold in original); these requirements extend to scholars in areas including physics (APS, 2008a), psychology (APA, 2002), and other research fields. Professional engineers, like others who conduct contract work for private, governmental, or other organizations, must clarify all statements "by explicitly identifying the interested parties on whose behalf they are speaking, and by revealing the existence of any interest the engineers may have in the matters" (NSPEPEI, 2007, Section II, ¶3c). Nurses giving treatment have obligations to guarantee that the "individual receives sufficient information on which to base consent for care and related treatment" (ICN, 2006, p. 2), and psychologists who administer mental health treatment carry similar obligations (APA, 2002). Any scholar conducting research with human participants—as many psychologists, nurses, and other researchers do—must fully inform participants of all risks, benefits, confidentiality precautions, and potential uses of data (see APA, 2002). These disparate requirements drive similar teaching behaviors among college and university instructors in these disciplines.

Students, much like research participants, clients, patients, employers, and other involved parties, must be informed and consenting participants in the educational process. First, this requires that students know the requirements of their various programs, including criteria for graduation, standards for quality, typical time requirements, and other obligations for successful completion of a thesis, dissertation, or license. Students, universities, and, indirectly, taxpayers benefit when students complete programs quickly and efficiently. Second, students should also receive realistic evaluations of their progress and likelihood of success in their programs. Although the academic and financial contributions of students, even those who do not graduate, can benefit academic programs, students should know the requirements and (to the degree that this is possible) have accurate expectations for success in their scholarly endeavors.

More concretely, in every class, university and college teachers must give each student accurate information about course topics, methods of evaluation, and the nature and other expectations of the course. A complete syllabus provides such information, and in twenty-first-century education a thorough syllabus has become a practical, ethical, and legal necessity that informs students and protects instructors (see McKeachie and Svinicki, 2005).

Relationships

All of the ethics codes discussed in this chapter lend guidance about human relationships. Many aspects of relationships have been explicitly or implicitly discussed here in dealing with competency, fairness, and informed consent, and this article returns to these ideas subsequently in discussions of confidentiality. This section addresses human relationships between instructors and students.

Concerns about inappropriate relationships exist across codes in history, physics, engineering, nursing, and psychology. Prohibitions against sexual harassment exist as explicit statements in some codes (AHA, 2007a, 2007b; APA, 2002; APS, 2008c), while other codes employ general statements regarding ethical treatment of co-workers (ICN, 2006) or requirements to follow applicable laws (NSPEPEI, 2006). These codes explicitly or implicitly prohibit quid pro quo sexual harassment (when a student's or employee's evaluation or other reward depends upon his or her responses to sexual advances from an instructor, employer, supervisor, or other individual with greater power). Additionally, the codes and relevant laws address hostile environment sexual harassment, which can occur when the educational or workplace environment itself poses difficulties for women or for men (see APS, 2008d, for a discipline-specific codified sample; see also U.S. Equal Opportunity Employment Commission, 2007, for relevant laws).

Beyond quid pro quo and hostile environment sexual harassment, the power differentials between instructors and students, advisees, and interns prohibit romantic relationships. Sexual relationships in these environments can cause severe damage to human lives, clearly to students but also to faculty, who may lose careers. The history of academia is loaded with tragic examples. To cite just one, despite his status as a former president of the American Psychological Association and his increasing eminence in the emerging behaviorism of the early 1900s, John B. Watson's academic career ended with his extramarital relationship with a graduate student (see Buckley, 1994; Cohen, 1979; King, Viney, and Woody, 2008). Similar events remain too likely in contemporary academia, and such events color public perceptions of universities and faculty alike (see Cahn, 1986); the costs for individuals and for academia as a whole are severe, particularly in hard-to-quantify areas such as lost public trust, potential decline in enrollment, and lost legislative and public willingness to allocate financial resources and political goodwill toward higher education.

Although sexual relationships are clearly problematic, nonsexual relationships can present difficulties as well (Keith-Spiegel, 1999). The existence of more than one professional or personal relationship between individuals can impose problems for teachers as well as health care providers. The APA (2002) code specifically defines multiple relationships for therapists or mental health providers, and these definitions extend to college and university instructors as well and encompass relationships not only with students but with students' family members or other associates, in the present and in the future. A multiple relationship exists if a teacher, advisor, mentor, or supervisor is "at the same time in another role with the [student]," if a teacher is "at the same time in a relationship with a person closely associated with or related to the [student]," or if a teacher "promises to enter into another relationship in the future with [the student] or a person closely associated with or related to the [student]" (APA, 2002, p. 1065). Despite these definitions, multiple relationships may pose particular difficulties for instructors at colleges or universities located in small communities or in communities that center on educational institutions. In this instance, teachers are likely to see students outside the classroom in social settings as well as in mundane settings such as gas stations, groceries, or other businesses.

Instructors face particular requirements to avoid students, when possible, in physical and mental health care settings to avoid breach of confidentiality. Professors who involve themselves in their campuses face other potential problems with multiple relationships, and the resulting issues may lead to complex questions. For example, can a professor in a nonmedical field who teaches yoga learn about a student's physical health problems to avoid injury in a yoga setting? Can a professor who unintentionally observes difficult interactions between a student and the student's family members separate these observations from class grades? Such extracurricular interactions may be unavoidable, and college and university instructors should work to separate, as much as possible, evaluation in the classroom from evaluation in other settings. In all cases, these relationships can affect an instructor's ability to preserve fairness for all students as well as the important public perceptions of the fairness of the instructor, his or her department, his or her university, and academia as a whole.

Even within appropriate professional relationships, other factors remain paramount to ethical instruction. When advising students who are assistants, interns, or collaborators in research, publication credit can raise difficult questions, particularly given the importance that academic administrators place on authorship and order of authorship in scholarly products. Instructors must remain aware of the power differential between themselves and students, discuss authorship early in the project, and assign authorship fairly and equitably in such a way that recognizes input from all contributors (AHA, 2007a; APA, 2002; APS, 2008a). Similar requirements to appropriately acknowledge input from others apply to practicing engineers (NSPE, 2007). Instructors, mentors, and advisors must not appropriate students' work for the instructor's own benefit, despite administrative or other professional rewards that may result (see Woody, 2004, 2008). Practitioners face additional requirements; nurses and other physical and mental health care professionals may share responsibility for patient care and therefore the responsibility to prevent errors not only on their part but also by co-workers (see ICN, 2006). Across all settings, concern for appropriate rewards for student input and protections for students and those to whom instructors and students owe responsibilities remain paramount; students learn as teachers explicitly address these questions, and students learn as they watch faculty model appropriate behavior in a variety of relationship contexts.

Confidentiality

Concerns regarding appropriate use and nondisclosure of information exist across the ethics codes discussed in this article. Historians have requirements to protect confidential sources, use information according to the limitations dictated by sources, and inform readers of these limits (AHA, 2007a). These expectations extend to students (AHA, 2007a), as will be discussed shortly. Professional engineers face broad confidentiality requirements; they "shall not disclose, without consent, confidential information concerning the business affairs or technical processes of any present or former client or employer, or public body on which they serve" (NSPE, 2007, ¶11). Nurses must protect confidentiality of patients, and the code recommends continued education in these questions for currently practicing nurses as well as newly trained nurses (ICN, 2006). Like nurses, psychologists (particularly those who are practitioners in mental health fields) must meet state and federal mandates for confidentiality in addition to discipline-specific codes (APA, 2002). Confidentiality requirements extend to teachers in higher education.

Daily classroom, mentorship, and advising activities require college and university instructors to protect students' confidentiality; some exceptions are discussed later. Protection of students' information requires several specific in-class behaviors. Although the APA allows some exceptions during the education of future counselors and group therapy facilitators (see APA, 2002), teachers cannot require excessive public disclosure of personal information in class. Instructors must protect students' personal information, including identifying details (e.g., student number, financial status, and so forth), academic records, and all class grades or other evaluative information. Instructors cannot post grades in public locations; public locations include physical locations such as a professor's door as well as electronic locations such as a Website that can be viewed by all class members. Additionally, instructors must prevent students from viewing other students' grades and written evaluative comments when returning examinations. Some teachers use creative folding or other covering methods to distribute papers without allowing students to see what others have earned. Similar requirements extend beyond the end of the class itself. College and university teachers must confidentially and securely store all student records for the period of time defined by institutional requirements. At the end of the required storage period, instructors must shred these records. Failure to maintain confidentiality can cause legal, academic, and other professional consequences. Beyond the classroom, instructors may not disclose students' information or evaluations with any parties who do not have legitimate university interests; there are, however, exceptions to these confidentiality requirements.

FERPA

The Family Educational Rights and Privacy Act or FERPA (see U.S. Department of Education, 2007a) presents parents or adult students (or students who are not eighteen but in a school beyond high school) with rights to access educational information and maintain confidentiality of such information. The conjunction "or" in the preceding sentence reflects the transfer of these rights from the parents of a child under eighteen who is in high school or earlier schooling to the adult child who is eighteen or beyond high school. Therefore, university and college instructors by definition interact with students who control their own academic information and can withhold information from their parents or allow their parents to access information at the student's own discretion (FERPA, 2007a). Exceptions exist, and FERPA guidelines (FERPA, 2007b) allow universities to "disclose educational records to parents if the student is a dependent for income tax purposes" (p. 2), if the student "is under age twenty-one and has violated any law or [the school's] policy concerning the use or possession of alcohol or a controlled substance" (p. 2), or in health or safety emergencies as discussed later. In many cases, professors do not know a student's status on his or her parents' tax return, and therefore instructors should avoid discussing a student's records with parents without an explicit guarantee from administrators having access to financial or other records that talking to the student's parents is appropriate in this case. Health and safety concerns raise other issues.

FERPA allows instructors and administrators to conduct typical university business by allowing evaluation of student transcripts by groups involved in financial aid, other "school officials with legitimate educational interest" in the student (U.S. Department of Education, 2007a, ¶6), and interuniversity exchange of academic information to evaluate transfer students. Despite the vagueness inherent in "legitimate educational interest," these requirements remain compatible with the previous paragraphs and with FERPA. College and university instructors, however, may breach confidentiality in some cases as discussed earlier and must do so in others. As late as 2000, universities won lawsuits by arguing that they do not owe students a duty to prevent suicide; more recently, however, universities (notably MIT) have settled out of court to avoid taking similar cases to trial (see Wolnick, 2007, for a review). FERPA outlines provisions to allow disclosure of private information without the student's consent for "health and safety emergencies" (U.S. Department of Education, 2007a, ¶6), and these provisions allow instructors to breach confidentiality in cases in which a student states an intention to harm himself or herself or to harm others. Additionally, instructors—like nurses, psychologists, K-12 teachers, and others—should report child or elder abuse. In all of these situations, instructors should immediately contact law enforcement, mental health personnel, and, if appropriate, physical health providers on campus.

Not surprisingly, the balance of privacy and safety became a prominent topic of public debate after the April 2007 tragedies at Virginia Tech, and many academics have wondered how to appropriately navigate these challenging conflicts. The text of FERPA (U.S. Department of Education, 2007a, 2007b) offers limited guidance in situations that present greater complexity and uncertainty than what is discussed here. Simply put, in a situation where explicit guidelines are or appear to be insufficient, or in any situation in which an instructor has concern about the health or safety of a student or about a potential threat posed by a student to others, the instructor should contact campus security, law enforcement, medical, or psychological resources for guidance to protect herself or himself, other students, the institution, and fundamentally the student of concern.

Explicitly Teaching Ethics

Requirements to present students with education in ethics exist across disciplinary codes. Teachers of history, including K-12 teachers, college and university faculty, and nonacademic historical scholars, are encouraged to discuss the potential bias of historians, presentation of differing values across historical contexts, and ethical approaches to historical methodology, among other ethical considerations (AHA, 2007c). Physicists have expectations to offer "mentoring of students, postdoctoral researchers, and employees with respect to . . . professional and ethical standards . . . [as] a core responsibility for supervisors" (APS, 2008b, ¶4). Managers of nurses have expectations to "provide continuing education in ethical issues," and educators and researchers in nursing should "provide teaching and learning opportunities for ethical issues and decision making" (ICN, 2006, p. 5). Although codes for professional engineers do not explicitly address education in ethics, these ideas are implicit in the codes' requirements of honesty and integrity in all activities (NSPE, 2007; NSPEPEI, 2006). Psychologists are required to educate future practitioners and other students in professional ethical behavior (APA, 2002).

Despite this strong common ground, these ethics codes omit requirements to teach ethical teaching. Even with appropriate education in ethics that fits each discipline, future teachers may not learn or discuss the issues presented in this article. New faculty members as well as graduate student teachers may arrive in the college or university classroom without having a single class on ethics; among psychology graduate students, only 6 percent had taken an ethics course before teaching classes (Branstetter and Handelsman, 2000). Many administrators assume that students absorb ethical skills from advisors in a process that has been called "ethics by 'osmosis'" (Handelsman, 1986, p. 371). Although at least some interdisciplinary graduate courses and textbooks in college teaching incorporate ethical teaching throughout the curriculum (see Davis, 1993; and McKeachie and Svinicki, 2005; among others), many college and university instructors do not have explicit education in ethical teaching, and observing ethical teachers, although critical, is not sufficient for educating future ethical teachers. These important topics must be central in development of future teachers and ongoing development of current instructors for the sake of today's students, tomorrow's teachers, and public perceptions of academia.

The Larger Historical Context

Too often, college and university instructors perceive themselves within the administrative confines of their positions. They may not perceive the larger historical and philosophical contexts in which they work. Many forces led to development of the current university system in the Middle Ages, among them the need for greater structure in mentoring and learning relationships (see King, Viney, and Woody, 2008). Universities and colleges today, despite considerable differences that have emerged in the last nine hundred years, continue many of the older traditions with historical titles, robes, and doctoral hoods; more fundamentally, the system perpetuates the roles of teachers and students such that students accept physical, mental, and financial difficulties for the opportunity to metaphorically sit at the feet of a teacher. These traditions exist throughout the history of Western cultures and include the young men who sat at the feet of Socrates (Plato, 1961) and Abelard, who studied under and eventually surpassed his teacher William de Champeaux (see Abelard, 1972), among others. These approaches also exist throughout Eastern cultures (Frantzis, 1998; Yuan, 1993).

Across all of these disparate historical formats and the five discipline-specific ethics codes reviewed in this article, the primary responsibility of the teacher is to the student. The learner brings faith, hope, and trust in the teacher, even if these characteristics appear hidden behind evaluation committees, academic transcripts, and administrative policies; the teacher must respond with recognition of the student's integrity as a human. This recognition of each student must guide everything discussed here. Beyond all of the specific and general responsibilities of ethical teaching, the integrity of the student is central. For the sake of each student, each discipline, the culture as a whole, and each teacher, instructors must recognize the ethical requirements of their roles and embrace the notion that teachers succeed when their students surpass them.

Notes

1. The ethical dilemmas resulting from limited economic access to comprehensive and preventive health care for the nearly forty-five million Americans (see U.S. Department of Health and Human Services, 2007) without health insurance are beyond the scope of this article.
2. Bias is typically viewed as negative and acting against the interests of the target; however, instructors must also recognize that bias in a student's favor is as unacceptable as bias against a student.

References

Abelard, P. *Historia Calamitatum* (H. A. Bellows, trans.). New York: Macmillan, 1972. (Original work written ca. 1130 and published 1922.)

American Association of University Professors. "Controversy in the Classroom: A Statement Issued by the AAUP's Committee A on Academic Freedom and Tenure." Mar., 3, 2004. http://www.aaup.org/statements/SpchState/comaclass.htm.

American Historical Association. "Statement on Standards of Professional Conduct." 2007a. http://www.historians.org/pubs/Free/ProfessionalStandards.cfm.

American Historical Association. "Statement on Discrimination and Harassment in Academia." 2007b. http://www.historians.org/governance/pd/DiscriminationAndHarassment.cfm.

American Historical Association. "Benchmarks for Professional Development in Teaching of History as a Discipline." 2007c. http://www.historians.org/teaching/policy/benchmarks.htm.

American Physical Society. "Ethics and Values 02.2: APS Guidelines for Professional Conduct." 2008a. http://www.aps.org/policy/statements/02_2.cfm.

American Physical Society. "Ethics and Values 04.1: Treatment of Subordinates." 2008b. http://www.aps.org/policy/statements/04_1.cfm.

American Physical Society. "Ethics and Values 94.3: Policy on Equal Professional Opportunity." 2008c. http://www.aps.org/policy/statements/94_3.cfm.

American Physical Society. "Ethics and Values 88.1: Displays in the Workplace of Graphic Material Depicting Demeaning Images of Women." 2008d. http://www.aps.org/policy/statements/88_1.cfm.

American Physical Society. "Human Rights 00.4: Protection Against Discrimination." 2008e. http://www.aps.org/policy/statements/00_4.cfm.

American Psychological Association. "Ethical Principles of Psychologists and Code of Conduct." *American Psychologist,* 2002, *57,* 1060–1074.

Andersen, S. M., Moskowitz, G. B., Blair, I. V., and Nosek, B. A. "Automatic Thought." In A. W. Kruglanski and E. T. Higgins (eds.), *Social Psychology: Handbook of Basic Principles.* New York: Guilford Press, 2007.

Branstetter, S. A., and Handelsman, M. M. "Graduate Teaching Assistants: Ethical Training, Beliefs, and Practices." *Ethics and Behavior,* 2000, *10,* 27–50.

Buckley, K. W. "Misbehaviorism." In J. T. Todd and E. K. Morris (eds.), *Modern Perspectives on John B. Watson and Classical Behaviorism.* Westport, Conn.: Greenwood Press, 1994.

Cahn, S. M. *Saints and Scamps: Ethics in Academia.* Totowa, N.J.: Rowman and Littlefield, 1986.

Cizek, G. J. "Preventing, Detecting, and Addressing Academic Dishonesty." In W. Buskist and S. F. Davis (eds.), *Handbook of the Teaching of Psychology.* Malden, Mass.: Blackwell, 2006.

Cohen, D. *J. B. Watson: The Founder of Behaviorism.* London: Routledge and Kegan Paul, 1979.

Davis, B. G. *Tools for Teaching.* San Francisco: Jossey-Bass, 1993.

Finken, L. L. "Teaching Human Sexuality." In W. Buskist and S. F. Davis (eds.), *Handbook of the Teaching of Psychology.* Malden, Mass.: Blackwell, 2006.

Frantzis, B. K. *The Power of Internal Martial Arts: Combat Secrets of Ba Gua, Tai Chi, and Hsing-I.* Berkeley, Calif.: North Atlantic Books, 1998.

Friedrich, J., and Douglass, D. "Ethics and the Persuasive Enterprise of Teaching Psychology." *American Psychologist,* 1998, *53,* 549–562.

Gravois, J. "The Battle over Studies of Faculty Bias." *Chronicle of Higher Education,* Jan., 26, 2007. http://chronicle.com/weekly/v53/i21/21a00801.htm.

Handelsman, M. M. "Problems with Ethics Training by 'Osmosis.'" *Professional Psychology: Research and Practice,* 1986, *17,* 371–372.

Hester, M. P., and Paloutzian, R. F. "Psychology of Religion." In W. Buskist and S. F. Davis (eds.), *Handbook of the Teaching of Psychology.* Malden, Mass.: Blackwell, 2006.

International Council of Nurses. *The ICN Code of Ethics for Nurses.* Geneva, Switzerland: International Council of Nurses, 2006.

Keith-Spiegel, P. "Ethically Risky Situations Between Students and Professors Outside of the Classroom." In B. Perlman, L. I. McCann, and S. H. McFadden (eds.), *Lessons Learned: Practical Advice for the Teaching of Psychology.* Washington, D.C.: American Psychological Society, 1999.

Keith-Spiegel, P. C., Tabachnick, B. G., and Allen, M. "Ethics in Academia: Students' Views of Professors' Actions." *Ethics and Behavior,* 1993, *3,* 149–162.

King, D. B., Viney, W., and Woody, W. D. *A History of Psychology: Ideas and Context* (4th ed.). Boston: Allyn and Bacon, 2008.

Klein, A. "Worried on the Right and the Left." *Chronicle of Higher Education,* July 9, 2004. http://chronicle.com/weekly/v50/i44/44a02101.htm.

McKeachie, W. J., and Svinicki, M. *McKeachie's Teaching Tips: Strategies, Research, and Theory for College and University Teachers* (12th ed.). Boston: Houghton-Mifflin, 2005.

National Society of Professional Engineers: Professional Engineers in Industry. *Guidelines to Employment for Professional Engineers* (4th ed.). Alexandria, Va.: National Society for Professional Engineers: Professional Engineers in Industry, 2006. http://www.nspe.org/resources/documents/pei/guidelines_rev4.doc.

National Society of Professional Engineers. *Code of Ethics for Engineers.* 2007. http://www.nspe.org/ethics/eh1-code.asp.

Palladino, J. J., Hill IV, W. G., and Norcross, J. C. "Using Extra Credit." In B. Perlman, L. I. McCann, and S. H. McFadden (eds.), *Lessons Learned: Practical Advice for the Teaching of Psychology.* Washington, D.C.: American Psychological Society, 1999.

Plato. *The Collected Dialogues of Plato Including the Letters* (E. Hamilton and H. Cairns, eds.). Princeton, N.J.: Princeton University Press, 1961.

Simpson, K. "Sacred Cow of Tenure Laid Low?" *Denver Post*, June 9, 2005. http://www.denverpost.com/search/ci_0002760059.

Smith, D. "What You Need to Know About the New Code: The Chair of APA's Ethics Code Task Force Highlights Changes to the 2002 Ethics Code." *Monitor on Psychology*, 2003, *34*, 62–65.

Suinn, R. M. "Teaching Culturally Diverse Students." In W. J. McKeachie and M. Svinicki (eds.), *McKeachie's Teaching Tips: Strategies, Research, and Theory for College and University Teachers* (12th ed.). Boston: Houghton-Mifflin, 2005.

Tabachnick, B. G., Keith-Spiegel, P., and Pope, K. S. "Ethics of Teaching: Beliefs and Behaviors of Psychologists as Educators." *American Psychologist*, 1991, *46*, 506–515.

U.S. Department of Education. "Family Educational Rights and Privacy Act." Washington, D.C.: Family Policy Compliance Office. U.S. Department of Education, 2007a. http://www.ed.gov/policy/gen/guid/fpco/ferpa/index.html.

U.S. Department of Education. "Balancing Student Privacy and School Safety: A Guide to the Family Educational Rights and Privacy Act for Colleges and Universities." Washington, D.C.: Family Policy Compliance Office, 2007b. U.S. Department of Education. http://www.ed.gov/policy/gen/guid/fpco/brochures/postsec.pdf.

U.S. Department of Health and Human Services. "Every American Insured." U.S. Department of Health and Human Services, 2007. http://www.hhs.gov/everyamericaninsured/.

U.S. Equal Opportunity Employment Commission. "Sexual Harassment." Washington, D.C.: U. S. Equal Opportunity Employment Commission, 2007. http://www.eeoc.gov/types/sexual_harassment.html.

Van Note Chism, N. "Valuing Student Differences." In W. J. McKeachie and M. Svinicki (eds.), *McKeachie's Teaching Tips: Strategies, Research, and Theory for College and University Teachers* (11th ed.). Boston: Houghton Mifflin, 2001.

Ward, M. J., and Merves, E. S. "Full-time Freshmen with Disabilities Enrolled in 4-year Colleges: A Statistical Profile." 2006. http://www.heath.gwu.edu/archived/news letter/issue18/new_freshman_data.htm.

Wittig, A. F., and others. "Treating Students Differentially: Ethics in Shades of Grey." In B. Perlman, L. I. McCann, and S. H. McFadden (eds.), *Lessons Learned: Practical Advice for the Teaching of Psychology*. Washington, D.C.: American Psychological Society, 1999.

Wolnick, E. "Depression Discrimination: Are Suicidal College Students Protected by the Americans with Disabilities Act?" *Arizona Law Review*, 2007, *49*, 989–1016.

Woody, W. D. "Universities, Psychology Departments, and the Treatment of Graduate Students." In W. Buskist, V. W. Hevern, B. K. Saville, and T. Zinn (eds.), *Essays from Excellence in Teaching* (vol. 3). Electronic book: Society for the Teaching of Psychology, 2004. http://teachpsych.lemoyne.edu/teachpsych/eit/eit2003/index.html.

Woody, W. D. "Collaboration: Faculty Perspective." In R. Miller and others (eds.), *Developing, Promoting, and Sustaining the Undergraduate Research Experience in Psychology*. Electronic book: Society for the Teaching of Psychology, 2008. http://teachpsych.org/resources/e-books/ur2008/5-2%20Woody.pdf.

Yuan, Zhao Da. *Practical Chin Na: A Detailed Analysis of the Art of Seizing and Locking* (Cartmell, trans.). Orange, Calif.: Unique, 1993.

WILLIAM DOUGLAS WOODY *is associate professor of psychological sciences at the University of Northern Colorado. He has earned numerous national, university, and college teaching awards and has been named best professor by the students at two of the three universities where he has taught.*

NEW DIRECTIONS FOR HIGHER EDUCATION • DOI: 10.1002/he

5

A group of faculty, administrators, and students developed a code of ethics governing all members of a university community.

Thinking Through the Issues in a Code of Ethics

Michael Davis

One sunny Monday in June 2005, seven people met for lunch at the faculty club of the Illinois Institute of Technology (IIT). Bill Parks was a trustee, as well as a very senior alumnus. Greg Barrett was in Institutional Advancement, the administrative office responsible for enlarging IIT's endowment and therefore for making sure faculty get on well with alumni, especially with alumni who are also trustees. The other five participants were faculty. Bruce Fisher, an expert in focus groups, was at the Institute of Psychology (what most universities would call the psychology department). Jack Hartray, an architect, was a member of the advisory board of IIT's Center for the Study of Ethics in the Professions (CSEP). The other three—Robert Ladenson, Vivian Weil, and I—were also associated with CSEP. Though trained as philosophers, the three of us had some experience with codes of ethics for professions and business, especially their use in ethics training. Weil and I had also been involved in writing at least one code of ethics before.[1] But none of us—indeed, none of the seven—knew anything about writing a code of ethics for a university community. Few do—which is the reason I thought reporting what happened at IIT might be useful to others.

Parks was responsible for the meeting. Drawing on his experience in business and reading about recent scandals involving universities, he had asked the most recent trustees' meeting whether IIT had a code of ethics. An administrator had informed him that there was a code of ethics for students, that the faculty had the AAUP code of ethics, and that some administrative departments (such the Office of University Counsel) had a professional code. Parks responded that, good as this was, it was not the

New Directions for Higher Education, no. 142, Summer 2008 © Wiley Periodicals, Inc.
Published online in Wiley InterScience (www.interscience.wiley.com) • DOI: 10.1002/he.303

same as having a fundamental document for *everyone*. Having such a document was now standard business practice; it affords specificity beyond the directives of a brief Mission Statement and even merely aspirational Vision and Values Statement. Surely IIT should have such a code too, something to set an overall minimum standard for the institution.

Parks's response sufficed to make him a committee of one for exploring the possibility of such a code, with Barrett to assist. Barrett contacted CSEP, one of the world's oldest ethics centers and a leader in professional ethics in general and engineering ethics in particular. Weil, its director, called around, soon assembled what she thought would be a good start at an exploratory committee, and arranged lunch for the seven. After introductions, Parks repeated the comments he had made at the trustees' meeting, adding that he thought it was important to get a "starter draft" as soon as possible. He had searched the Web and was surprised that the only code of ethics for a university community he found was one that the University of Southern California (USC) had adopted the year before.[2] Although he did not care for the code because it sounded like the work of a university president, it inspired him to sketch one of his own, consisting merely of key ideas: integrity, academic excellence, academic freedom, mutual respect and dignity, pride, responsibility to neighborhood, personal responsibility, work-life concerns. There was immediate agreement on the need for a starter code. There was also immediate agreement that the starter code should be developed into a final code using a procedure of "wide consultation" (focus groups) both to determine what standard was actually needed and to get buy-in from the IIT community. The community was much more likely to accept a code that it actually developed, and the board of trustees was more likely to accept a code that came to it with wide support.

I undertook to prepare a starter draft, using Parks's key ideas. The faculty were to hold the first focus group, primarily because theirs seemed the easiest to arrange. After agreement on these matters, discussion ranged more widely. Drawing on her experience with professional societies, Weil noted that "wide consultation" was not only a way to achieve buy-in; it was also itself a way to educate a community in the purpose, content, and use of the code. Many professional societies found writing or revising the code an important lesson in ethics, a consciousness raising experience. Drawing on similar experience, I added that most people who participated in drafting a code bottom up were occasionally surprised by what ended up in the document. Ethical standards are, in part, created rather than simply documented. Involving the whole community takes advantage of a range of experience. Drawing on his business experience, Parks stressed that adopting the code was only a first step. The group should already be thinking about how to disseminate the code, how to keep it in mind in making decisions, how to guide its application, and how to correct those who violated it. Those remarks ended the business meeting, though several of the participants—Parks,

NEW DIRECTIONS FOR HIGHER EDUCATION • DOI: 10.1002/he

Hartray, and we three philosophers—reminisced for another half hour. (All of us had been associated with IIT for at least twenty years.) The process was launched.

First Draft

A few days after that meeting, I began work by writing a preamble. A preamble should, I thought, (1) state the reasons for having a code, (2) explain who is covered and why, and (3) present a rationale for everyone covered to do as the code requires. From my own theory of what codes of ethics do,[3] I soon had this paragraph:

> Having voluntarily chosen to associate ourselves with IIT, we—trustees, students, faculty, administrators, and staff—have become beneficiaries of what generations of trustees, students, faculty, administrators, and staff have made. We are also each a steward for this generation and for the generations to follow. For each of us, the benefit deriving from association with IIT depends on the conduct of others associated with IIT. If we each conduct ourselves as we should, all associated with IIT will have good reason for pride. If even a few fail to do as they should, we will all have reason for shame, the benefits of association will contract, and we will pass on to the next generation less than we might have. This code of ethics is intended to help us all conduct ourselves as we should.[4]

Next, I did my own Web search. That turned up one more code, Howard University's, adopted in 1998.[5] The Howard code was, at 2,747 words, about five times as long as USC's. Its language had something of the lawyer's caution about it, as well as a lawyer's care in thinking about how the code would be used. For example, the Howard code is divided into small sections, each on a single topic. The larger sections are titled. It is easy to find what one is looking for (and easy to cite it). In contrast, USC's code is just a series of paragraphs, none labeled and each containing several sentences. Often the sentences in a paragraph are on a topic only loosely related to other topics discussed in the same paragraph. Finding what one needs is much harder than in Howard's code, even though USC's code is much shorter.

I liked Howard's use of titles for another reason. People evaluating a code of ethics tend to look for certain words ("integrity," "honesty," "conflict of interest," "diversity," and so on). They are likely to reject a code if their favorite words do not appear. Many codes end up using those words without defining them, giving users of the code much less guidance than they could and should have. I thought we could use such words as titles to satisfy the desire to have those words appear in the code while using the text to define the relevant conduct.

Having concluded that Howard offered a better model for a useful code, I began turning Parks's key ideas into provisions of the IIT code by looking for appropriate language in Howard's code. Sometimes I found it. For example, the Howard code offered this language suited to filling out Parks's "academic freedom":

> No member of the University Community shall deny any member of the Faculty a fair opportunity to teach, [to] conduct research, and to provide services to the community, in a setting that provides the academic freedom necessary to cultivate a wide expanse of ideas and teaching methods [IV.E].

Though a good start, this provision had at least three failings. First, Howard used *academic freedom* to mean only the freedom of faculty, though there was a separate provision to protect students, which did not call the protection academic freedom:

> No member of the University Community shall deny a student fair access to all educational opportunities and benefits available at the University [IV.E].

There was no provision to protect the academic freedom of other members of the university community. The exploratory committee had agreed that all provisions of the IIT code should apply as widely as possible—and, in particular, that academic freedom belonged to everyone at IIT.

Second, Howard's provisions on academic freedom seemed unduly negative (as did the corresponding provisions of USC's code). Why not state the obligation positively (provided it can be done in a way that was neither opaque nor prolix)?

The third failing was perhaps even more important. IIT is an institute of technology, a university as much concerned with making as knowing. The freedom to "cultivate ideas and teaching methods" seemed entirely too narrow to protect the design of new things, writing of software, and carrying out of experiments that are central activities at IIT (and, indeed, at any modern university). Even in the realm of ideas, "exploration" is not the part of academic life that is most in need of protection. What most needs protection is developing new ideas and putting them into practice.[6]

With all this in mind, I rewrote the Howard provision to read:

> *Academic freedom.* We shall seek to ensure to every student a fair opportunity to learn, to every faculty member a fair opportunity to teach, and to every member of the community a fair opportunity to explore human invention in research, design, scholarship, politics, religion, and art.

Howard's code was a useful starting point for filling out Parks's term *academic freedom*. But for some of Parks's key ideas, there was no counterpart in

Howard's code, or USC's. I had to work from scratch. So, for example, "academic excellence" became:

> Because IIT's reputation depends in large part on the quality of the students it graduates, research it performs, and scholarship it publishes, we shall do what we can to help students, faculty, and researchers do the best work they can—and to attract to IIT those who can do even better.

Once I was done, I had a document about the length of USC's, consisting of a preamble and nine one-sentence paragraphs, each titled and numbered. I labeled it Version 1. After letting it sit for a few days, I decided it was the best I could do without further guidance and e-mailed it to the other members of the exploratory committee. There were several suggestions for improvements. I responded with Version 1.1 (adopting the numbering typical of software) and again circulated the draft. A few more suggestions yielded Version 1.2 (September 22, 2005). When I circulated that draft, Weil made two additions on her own, yielding 1.3 (September 29).[7] The first draft was ready for the first focus group.

First Focus Group: Faculty

Finding enough faculty for the focus group proved difficult. The problem was not finding enough of IIT's faculty of three hundred willing to participate but finding enough of them free at the same time. The meeting did not occur until November 30. There were ten members of the faculty present, including one department chair and several full professors. Fisher presided; I was present to answer questions (and to listen). CSEP's librarian took extensive notes (as she would for all focus groups to come).

After describing the process of drafting Version 1.3, Fisher stated the purpose of the meeting and laid out the procedures: "We want you to raise ethical issues you might confront."[8] These were not to be stated abstractly but in the form of brief, realistic "scenarios." Given the time available, eleven would be enough. For each scenario, the group would find a response, state a "guideline" that underlay that response, and then see whether the guideline was already present in the code or should be added. Fisher, as a business consultant who had done many focus groups, expected to lead an orderly discussion, moving from one scenario to another, each discussion taking about ten minutes (including the discussion of the relevant guideline).[9] He soon learned that professors are (as the Germans say) "people who think otherwise."

The first response to Fisher's statement of ground rules was a question from the one law professor present: "What is the ultimate purpose of the code?" Fisher responded that the code was "designed as a guide to understand certain issues." A professor from the Institute of Design (ID) added helpfully, "Moral requirements." An engineer then asked, "Is it reflected in the code of ethics? Most issues in the draft do not seem to be ethical issues." The professor from ID then offered more help: "Ethics is morality. These are special standards which go beyond morality." And so the discussion went, for perhaps fifteen minutes. Fisher intervened when a math professor began to complain about the administration's treatment of his department: "This is a scenario where the administration dictated." The math professor agreed, "Stay and merge. Maintain standards of mathematics." Fisher then offered a guideline that might state the underlying principle on which the math professor was acting: "You did not quit but worked for the wellbeing of your students." The math professor responded, "This did not cross my mind." For him, the standards of mathematics were what counted.

Though this exchange seemed to have gone nowhere, in fact it brought the discussion back to scenarios. There followed a discussion of "whistle blowing" (going outside IIT to complain about policy or particular decisions, in this case merging mathematics with computer science). Then the discussion returned to the question of whom the code would cover, the law professor asking whether "donors are part of the ethics group." Fisher then added "alumni." No one objected, though neither of these groups was listed in 1.3 (or in either USC's code or Howard's).

Fisher then pointed out that he had hoped to have the faculty focus on issues they faced, not issues donors or alumni faced. Another engineer described a scenario in which senior faculty mistreated a new hire. The discussion of that scenario led back to whistle blowing. And so it went. Though far less orderly than Fisher (or anyone else in the exploratory committee) had expected, the meeting ended with my having a long list of issues clearly not covered in 1.3: not only whistle blowing and defining the IIT community as including donors and alumni but also confidentiality, misuse of software, responsibility for ensuring adequate resources for instruction, the place of "integrity," and so on. But whistle blowing was clearly the most important issue. It had surfaced again and again, taking up perhaps a third of the meeting's more than two hours.

Version 2. The next morning I sat before my computer with my notes of the meeting and remembered bits of discussion not represented in the notes. There were many suggestions for small changes throughout, some significant enough to require a new paragraph, but nothing (it seemed) to require a change in format. I began with the preamble, adding "donors" and "alumni" to the list of those the code covered (since no one objected to their inclusion), making the order of community members alphabetical (though no one had noticed that I had—inadvertently—put "staff" at the end of the reverse alphabetical list instead of just after "trustees," where the alphabet directed). I also tried to make the preamble clearer, shortening it as I did.[10] There had been too many questions about what the purpose of the code was.

I initially tried to respond to the list of missing provisions by adding new sections or inserting new phrases in existing provisions. In some cases, this worked well. For example, I added a new paragraph 3 (renumbering the others):

Academic Responsibility. We shall maintain appropriate standards of accuracy, reliability, credit, candor, and confidentiality in our own work, whether for publication or internal use in class or office.

This one provision took care of a surprisingly large number of concerns the faculty had raised.

But I soon realized that simply adding or amending provisions would not always work. As I looked over what I had done, I saw an underlying pattern in some of the changes. So, for example, 1.3's paragraph 3 (now 4) was:

Diversity of Thought, Culture, Gender, and Ethnicity. Because we recognize the contribution to education, research, and scholarship that differences in perspective, experience, and history offer, we shall seek to maintain an environment in which those differences may both flourish individually and combine productively in common projects.

Although the term *diversity* today has a cultural, gender, or ethnic emphasis (or some combination of them), it has not always had it and probably will not always, as today's bigotry goes the way of earlier kinds. However, the underlying problem of diversity, the one a code of ethics should address, will remain. People have a tendency to be hostile to differences from which they can in fact benefit, especially difference in attitude, style, or commitment. Part of respecting people is respecting such differences. So, 1.3's paragraph 4 (now 5: Mutual Respect and Human Dignity) could be a subparagraph under 4, as could a provision I had just written about the importance of respecting dissent (designed to make protecting whistle blowers a special case of protecting diversity). Realizing this, I decided to violate the format I had adopted.[11] Below paragraph 4 (its title shortened to "Diversity"), I put two subparagraphs:

4.1. Mutual Respect and Human Dignity. Because every member of the IIT community deserves that minimum respect due every human being, we shall try to treat every member of the IIT community fairly, avoiding harassment, unjust discrimination, and intimidation in our own conduct and not tolerating them in the conduct of others.

4.2. Community and Criticism. Because opinions in any healthy community tend to differ, with wisdom never anyone's monopoly, we shall consult those associated with IIT whom our decisions may affect, shall suggest to appropriate persons opportunities for improving IIT when we think we see them, offering our suggestions in ways unlikely to distract from their merit, shall accept the dissent of others from our views as an opportunity to learn, and shall protect dissenters from mistreatment their dissent seems to have provoked.

A similar analysis suggested that paragraph 5 (Personal Responsibility) could also have two subparagraphs under it, one concerned with whistle blowing (Responsibility for the Conduct of Others) and another for conscientious objection (Legal Liability and Conscience). These changes, though together sufficient to justify calling the draft Version 2.0, were easily completed in two days (that is, by December 2).

Oddly, there were again nine main paragraphs (though two now had subparagraphs). When no one in the exploratory committee found anything to object to, Version 2.0 became the document laid before the next focus group, administrators. Their meeting did not occur until February 15, 2006.

Administrators' Focus Groups. There were eleven people present at the administrators' focus group: Fisher (who again presided), two deans (who held faculty rank), several vice presidents without faculty rank (among them the chief financial officer), and three lower-ranking administrators without academic rank (such as the assistant dean for academic administration).

Fisher began the meeting by stating the purpose of the code, describing the process until then and the purpose of the meeting, and giving much the same description of the meeting's procedure that he had given the faculty.

The administrators immediately began to ask questions the faculty had not: Is this a new document or a revision of something IIT already has? Why have a unifying code? Why has the president not been engaged in this conversation (rather than merely notified of it)? What is the relation between the code and the mission, vision, and values statements the administration is working on? And so on.

Once Fisher had answered these stage-setting questions (or at least agreed to look for answers), the administrators turned to the code itself. There were again the questions the faculty had asked: "What is ethics?" and "What is a code of ethics?" Fisher had answers ready this time. "Ethics is a standard of excellence" (something beyond ordinary morality), and a code of ethics states those special standards.

That seemed to satisfy the administrators on the points raised, but the meeting was not yet on track. "In the opening paragraph," one administrator noted, "[it says], 'If even a few fail to do as they should, we will all have reason for shame.' This phrase is like something out of third grade and should be rephrased." After that comment was duly noted, the administrators fell to work, doing pretty much what Fisher had asked of them. They briefly described ten ethically troubling scenarios (all, apparently, drawn from life) and then stated for each an "ethical guideline" that resolved it. The first (and shortest) of the problem-solution exercises may serve as a sample of them all:

> A group starts a project and fails to sufficiently notify top members of the administration.

Ethical Guidelines:

All members of the university community should be notified of programs/ projects that might involve or influence them.

Though the administrators made no effort to connect their "ethical guidelines" with Version 2, most of their guidelines in fact corresponded to something in the code. For example, the notification guideline corresponded to 4.2. Indeed, 4.2 actually required more, not just notification but consultation ("Because opinions in any healthy community tend to differ, with wisdom never anyone's monopoly, we shall consult those associated with IIT whom our decisions may affect").

Version 2 generally passed most of the tests that the administrators' scenarios set, but in one case it clearly did not. The administrators agreed that it is "fine to complain internally, but not externally." Even though many faculty members may not see it that way, external whistle blowing is, they thought, an ethical issue. IIT's welfare may be at stake. Or, as one administrator put it: "Many people at IIT do not have pride in the university, and often will complain publicly about IIT at conferences, to visitors, and even to new students, faculty, and staff. In some cases, [a] faculty [member] has even complained to students about [the] university [in a way] that can lead to drops in donor gifts and . . . IIT's institutional standing. Word of mouth is very powerful in [the] status of a university."

Because the code seemed, in general, to deal adequately with the administrators' scenarios, the revisions that followed were small, yielding Version 2.1 (February 28). That Version differed from 2 in two ways (apart from correction of some typographical errors). First, the preamble was shortened by deleting the "third grader's language" about shame ("we will all have reason for shame; the benefits of association will be less; and"). Second, a sentence was added to paragraph 9: "We shall not take complaints about IIT outside until we have given those at IIT a fair opportunity to resolve them properly." (Of course, that addition violated the one-sentence-per-paragraph format, opening the flood gates.)

I then e-mailed 2.1 to the exploratory committee, expecting general approval. I was surprised when Ladenson, with whom I almost always agree, e-mailed back that he had a problem with 5.2 (Legal Liability and Conscience), a paragraph one might have expected the administrators to object to if there were anything to object to ("Should we believe our use of IIT resources morally right but illegal, we may do what we think morally right, provided we ensure IIT does not thereby suffer legal liability or other substantial harm"). Ladenson, a lawyer as well as a philosopher, thought this provision gave too much freedom to individual conscience. He initially suggested dropping the provision altogether but relented when reminded of the faculty discussion that had inspired it. Because Ladenson considered it a make-or-break issue, he suggested that we three philosophers meet informally to see whether we could work something out. After that meeting, I cast the ideas discussed there into a provision with a heavy emphasis on procedure. The new provision did not satisfy Ladenson, though his concern now was making the point clearer. In the end, we three philosophers agreed on this language for 5.2:

> Should we believe our use of IIT resources right but illegal, we shall consult appropriate legal authority to confirm that belief, to explore legal alternatives, and to define legal consequences. If, after consulting the appropriate legal authority, we still believe the use of resources is right but illegal, we may act on that belief, provided IIT will suffer neither legal liability nor other substantial harm as a result.

This change from Version 2 seemed (together with a lot of tinkering with punctuation and other small changes) to justify naming the resulting document Version 3 (March 28). That was the version the students' focus group would examine.

Students' Focus Group. Nine students met on April 18, 2006, to discuss Version 3, a student (a member of the student government) presiding. The students did not worry about scenarios. Instead, they were the first focus group to examine the code line by line. They found much they liked. For example, one student's response to the preamble was: "It is a good idea to [recognize] that ethics is not imposed from the outside but it starts from inside, from human nature." But in general, they focused on what they thought should be changed. For example, although they agreed that the preamble should explain why the code should be followed, they did not like the preamble's giving "pride" as a reason to follow the code. One student even found the word "offensive." They suggested dropping "pride" in favor of "having the satisfaction of doing what is right." So they proceeded, through each paragraph and subparagraph.

The students did not just comment but debated interpretations, cooperated in devising alternate language, and often reached consensus. Their discussions were both lively and free of deference. Consider, for example, their response to the language of 5.2 with which Ladenson, Weil, and I had just taken such pains (Legal Liability and Conscience). The discussion began with a suggestion: "We should either put in the example of software or broaden the wording to include more issues." Perhaps illustrating the problem, another student asked, "When 5.2 says 'right,' what is the right? Does 'right' mean if we are using copyrighted software illegally to spread a cure for cancer, or something else?" The discussion continued along this path for a few minutes. Then one student noted, "In no place in the document is the word 'integrity' used. We could use it in this section to clarify it." That gave another student an idea: "What if we delete what is in 5.2

entirely and label it, '5.2 Integrity' and add a new sentence? We may want to use integrity instead of pride in the preamble, as well." To this someone responded, "5.2 does not seem to fit in this document. The rest of the code lays down principles, but 5.2 reads like a code of conduct and gives exact instructions on what to do in a certain situation. Can we rewrite [it] to sound like a code of ethics rather than 'if this, then this'?"

The discussion concluded: "Let's scratch 5.2 and put in its place . . . anything?" Clearly, revision 5.2 was in trouble.

When I first saw the minutes of the student meeting, I was both surprised and disappointed. Among the surprises was the rejection of the term *pride* (though the substitution the students proposed seemed good enough). Among the disappointments was the rejection of 5.2 after a discussion that, given the software example, showed the students understood the provision. I personally had no objection to some provisions of a code of ethics giving exact instructions while others were general. A code, I thought, should embody as much specificity as could be agreed on so long as the language was unlikely to be outdated in a few years.

But as I went over the minutes more carefully with Version 3 before me, my response changed. Here was the first close reading a focus group had given the code. Many of the student comments were just first responses, with other comments either rejecting or modifying them. Though the first comment often involved a misreading of a provision, the discussion quickly reached what I considered a proper interpretation. The students had in fact shown that the code was relatively easy to use. In addition, many of the suggestions the students made were helpful, especially those concerned with titling and organization. Some, of course, were not. For example, I thought the suggestion to put "students" first rather than in alphabetical order would open up a debate about which group was more important than which—one that, though having nothing to do with the substance or use of the code, could well arouse strong emotions and threaten the code's adoption. Who would come second? Who third? And so on.

I took only a few days to produce Version 4 (April 24) and 4.1 (May 12). They differed from Version 3 in only small or middle-sized ways (organization, titles, use of "try" throughout rather than mixing "try" with "seek," and so on). The result was a document of eight main paragraphs (instead of nine), but of about the same length (because one paragraph had become a subparagraph). Informal discussion among the three philosophers suggested a new subparagraph under 5 concerning conflict of interest. That change yielded Version 4.3 (June 22).

Version 4.4 followed a day later when I realized that every focus group had begun in much the same way, with participants asking what a code of ethics was and how to use it. Why not, I wondered, offer answers in the code itself? That such an explanation was a rarity in codes did not matter.[12]

Clearly, such an explanation was needed—a new paragraph entitled "How to Use This Code." I attached a sort of "post-amble" or epilogue:

> This code consists of a preamble and eight sections. The preamble explains the purpose of the code and provides a principle for applying the general rules in the eight sections to specific situations (interpret the rules so as to pass on to our successors an IIT at least as good as we found it). Some sections include subsections. The rules in these subsections provide a *partial* interpretation of the section's general rule. Each subsection provides a reminder of a domain of conduct requiring special care. This code is not a moral algorithm, a substitute for deliberation, or an ordinary regulation, designed for external enforcement, but a guide to conscience in deliberation. It captures what we now believe is how we would like other members of the IIT community to act. It is, of course, subject to revision in light of experience.

I put the explanation at the end of the code rather than at the beginning because I thought someone using the code would be more likely to pay attention to it after reading the code (or relevant provisions) and developing questions about interpretation. I did not want to discourage reading through the code by making readers plow through the explanation before they had questions it answered.

Ladenson, Weil, and I agreed that something should be done about the troublesome 5.2 (besides renaming, moving, and renumbering it—all of which I had done), but they could not agree on what that was. A flurry of e-mails and informal conversations ended with Ladenson in favor of cutting the clause entirely and my arguing (as the students had) that something was needed. The code was as ready as it was going to be for the next focus group.

The Trustee's Focus Group—and the Staffs'

On July 20, Weil met with seven members of IIT's board of trustees (about a fifth of the board). Like the student meeting, this one focused on the code itself, not on scenarios. Unlike the student meeting, the trustees did not have the latest version. The version they discussed, the one they had been sent a month before the meeting, was 4.3 (without 4.4's how-to paragraph).[13] This, however, does not seem to have much affected the discussion. The trustees did not ask what a code of ethics is. They seem to have had no doubt they knew—perhaps relying on their experience in business.

Experience with business codes may have produced its own problems, though. For example, the discussion of paragraph 1 began with a trustee observing that academic excellence "is not an ethical matter; it is an academic matter." Later the same trustee asked, "[Is] helping people do the best they can an ethical or performance issue?" There was general agreement that it was a performance issue, "an institutional issue but not an ethical issue." After considerably more discussion of the first paragraph, one of the trustees summarized the consensus: "Re-wordsmith Item 1 to reflect changes suggested: . . . 1. Change title to "Environment of Academic Excellence"; 2. Add "character" after "quality" in first section ["IIT's reputation depends in large part on the quality *and character* of students it graduates"]; 3. Change last sentence [or, rather, clause] to "we shall provide an environment where students, faculty, and researchers can excel." They then moved on to the next paragraph.[14]

Overall, the trustees' discussion, though considerably more structured than the students', was otherwise similar. They worked their way through the code, paragraph by paragraph (leaving the preamble to last). They suggested many changes, usually quite specific. Some were clearly right. For example, they suggested adding "suppliers" to the list of members of the IIT community. Many of the suggestions were stylistic. The trustees regularly tried to break long sentences into several shorter ones (to make the code easier to read). In this too, they were probably right. Disagreements with the substance of the code were few. The most important concerned the ever-troublesome personal integrity provision (what had been "Legal Liability and Conscience"). The trustees reached much the same conclusion as the students: "This is a concept that is needed in the code. A paragraph is needed, but the current paragraph is not it."

In two respects, however, the trustees broke new ground. First, they concluded their meeting with a long discussion of what was going to be done with the code. They had many ideas: ask "staff, students, suppliers, etc. . . . to sign the code"; ask "IIT community members . . . to sign a waiver saying they read the code"; "create a code of conduct that is a derivative of the IIT Code of Ethics that is signed"; have the code "distributed and enforced among trustees, students staff, faculty administration, alumni, and suppliers"; and having it "printed in some sort of dignified pocket-sized fold-out card and made available to students during recruitment."

The other respect in which the trustees broke new ground was a change in procedure. They instructed the CSEP librarian (who took notes of the meeting) to prepare a draft reflecting their decisions. This the librarian did, titling it "Changes to Rough Draft 4.3 by Trustee Focus Group (July 20, 2006)." For brevity, I shall call it "4.3T."

Version 4.3T is a disordered work. Though the preamble has "suppliers" inserted between "alumni" and "administrators" (out of alphabetical order), it also has a tenth numbered paragraph that has the same effect ("It is our expectation that all supply chain partners will uphold the same ethical standards as we uphold ourselves."). The troublesome personal integrity paragraph has become a fill-in-the-blank: "6. Personal integrity. (Something similar to) Each individual will behave. . . ." And so on. Committees are notoriously poor writers.

I saw the minutes of the trustees' meeting, but I did not see Version 4.3T. Working from 4.4, I produced a document differing from it in only small ways, but enough, I thought, to deserve the title "Version 5" (July 26).

The most important change (apart from adding "suppliers" to the preamble and paragraph 9) was the substitution of "should" for a variety of equivalents ("is intended to," "shall," "shall try to," and so on).

The Last Focus Group

Nothing much happened in August until Weil called a meeting of the exploratory committee. It met on September 1, with only Weil, Ladenson, and the CSEP librarian present. (Fisher and I were out of town.)[15] The discussion focused on Fisher's dissatisfaction with Version 5.0, apparently expressed in a memo to Weil that has not survived. But a few days after this meeting (September 6), Fisher e-mailed the exploratory committee a version of 5.0 (oddly named "54.0") with his comments. Fisher's overall complaint was that I "did not capture the input of the various interview groups." For example, "the order of stakeholders is important—too important to just go in reverse alphabetical order: students should come first." Fisher was especially unhappy with the Personal Integrity provision:

> I don't remember any of this in the interviews. It seems odd to me to publicly support taking illegal action based on what could be a unique view of morality. I know integrity was viewed as important by interview groups, and I agree that it should be a tenant [sic]. I believe it was represented more as a function of doing what they say they will do (walking the talk), keeping commitments to others, and such. I also remember a lot of discussion about the importance of transparency in decisions and processes to enable people to understand what the university is doing and why it's doing it.[16]

Though the exploratory committee (or, at least, a fragment of it) had a long and thorough discussion of the issues Fisher raised, it did not reach a decision on anything. They did not even discuss the new how-to paragraph.

After reading the minutes of the exploratory committee and looking over the comments on Version 5, I made a few changes and sent out Version 5.1 (September 6). Fisher repeated his earlier objections after asking for a version of 5.1 showing changes. Weil was now quite worried. The whole process depended on consensus. If one of the exploratory committee's members dissented strongly enough, the whole process might collapse. She therefore called another meeting of the committee, one Fisher and I could attend. On September 28, we met. The meeting began rather roughly. After Fisher explained his objections, I explained my method. My job was not simply to do whatever one of the focus groups said to do, but to produce a coherent document that everyone would find satisfactory. So, for example, I had not put the students first in the list of community members because that sort of symbolism invited controversy and made absolutely no substantive difference. Of course, there were problems with the code as it stood, the most important of which was certainly the personal integrity paragraph (now numbered 6). But, I continued, the focus groups had not had any problem with my original language; the troubles had begun with the language that the exploratory committee had, at Ladenson's urging, put in its place. I would not do what Fisher asked; I would not be "a mere scribe." If the exploratory committee wanted a mere scribe, I would be happy to quietly quit the committee. Because even Fisher did not want that, the meeting ended without any decision about Version 5.1.

Finding staff for a focus group proved complicated, but toward the end of October Weil informed the exploratory committee that she had found enough participants and they would meet in November. I then sent Weil another version of the code, 5.2, differing from 5.1 primarily in breaking a few more long sentences into shorter ones (as the trustees had suggested) and substituting "we" in several places where "IIT community" had appeared before.

When the staff focus group met on November 16, 2006, seven staff were there (including the CSEP librarian). They included both relatively high-ranking staff (an associate director) and relatively low-ranking ones (a campus police officer, an employee of the security firm policing the campus). The version the staff discussed was "5.5"—not a variant of my last draft (5.2), but of the trustees' 4.3T that Weil prepared a day before the meeting. She reached back to the trustees' draft because it was the last version of the code to which more than one person had agreed. She did not simply use 4.3T but included some text from 4.3 and added several questions to guide discussion. So, for example, where the trustees' version left the personal integrity paragraph with a blank to fill, Weil gave the language of 4.3 but posed a question: "The preceding focus groups had problems with the wording of this provision. So far we have not found wording that is acceptable. What do you think about this provision?"

The staff approached 5.5 much as the faculty, administrators, and students had approached earlier versions. They asked about the purpose of a code. In particular, they wanted answers to such questions as this: "If I should go out at three in the morning to go drinking and have an accident, how much would that have to do with my employment in IIT? Is that covered by the code?" The staff wanted a code that was "aspirational" rather than "punitive." Once they got beyond these overall comments, they examined the code paragraph by paragraph (as the students and trustees had). Many of their comments concerned style. So, for example, the staff suggested revising the last sentence of the preamble ("This code of ethics is intended to help us all act as we should") to read "something like": "This code of ethics is intended to help us conduct ourselves with honesty and integrity." Some comments were substantive. For example, they suggested adding a new sentence to paragraph 4: "Every member of the IIT community deserves the respect due every person regardless of the individual's status or title." They thought it important that "equal levels of respect should be highlighted."

The personal integrity provision troubled them as it had everyone else. On the one hand, they rejected the current wording: "This one makes no sense. Who says what is morally right? All subjective. How do you define what is morally right? If IIT as an institution starts doing this, then [it will] fall into the trap of defining integrity for its community members."

On the other hand, all the staff could suggest to replace the offending words were variants of fill-in-the-blank, that is, either "Each individual needs to use their personal discretion . . ." or "Do what an ordinarily prudent person would do." They did not want to drop the provision entirely.

I found reading the minutes of the staff focus group unsettling. The staff seemed to have gone through the code as carefully as the students had, but they seemed to have missed much I had added to the code since the version the students had used. I was especially concerned that they had asked questions about the code that the final how-to paragraph was supposed to answer (something the trustees had not done). I did not notice that the version the staff discussed was 5.5 rather than one of mine. I supposed I was still the code's draftsman when in fact that function had passed to Weil and the CSEP librarian (perhaps without their realizing it). Nonetheless, I did not revise my draft in response to the staff meeting. Instead, I was thinking of quitting the exploratory committee.

The next focus group, scheduled for December 12, was to be the last. It consisted of a few people from each of the other focus groups, as well as Ladenson, the CSEP librarian, and me. Weil presided. The group was to give the code a final "once over." The meeting began with some confusion. Weil passed out a copy of "the code" (5.5)—a copy of which she had sent to all members of the focus group in advance. The first question, from the university counsel, was about the code's relationship to university policy. I responded that the group should look at the final paragraph for an answer. Everyone turned to the code's second page. The final paragraph was paragraph 9 (Sense of Pride and Ownership). The how-to paragraph wasn't there. I then looked more closely at the document before me and realized it was not my 5.2 but something quite different. I asked why the group did not receive the latest version of the code, the one with all the improvements. Weil explained. I must have looked horrified because Weil was soon sending the CSEP librarian back to CSEP to make copies of 5.2 for distribution. In the meantime, the group discussed what to do next with the code.

The librarian soon returned. Once she distributed copies of 5.2, there was a brief period in which everyone read. Then someone commented that 5.2 seemed to be "more finished" (that is, it did not include any questions or comments). Without any further discussion, the group began discussing 5.2. It was again a line-by-line discussion. But for the most part, the changes suggested were few and small (for example, moving a phrase in the how-to paragraph from one place to another). Finally, the discussion reached the troublesome personal integrity paragraph. Again there was agreement that something must be said on the subject, but no agreement on what. The university counsel was especially concerned that nothing in the code should even suggest illegality. Just when it seemed that the meeting would end without an overall endorsement of the code, Ladenson suggested a radical revision:

> 6. *Supporting personal integrity.* If we become aware of anyone associated with IIT who perceives a conflict between personal convictions and what is required under IIT's rules, we should help identify ways to arrive at a reasonable and just resolution.

This language satisfied everyone. The meeting adjourned with agreement that the code should be revised to take account of the day's discussion, we should have someone in technical writing look it over for readability, and we should then begin the process of approval. I had Version 6.0 ready three days later (December 15).

End Game

The professor of technical writing, someone who had no other part in writing the code, gave her approval on February 9: "[The] code is clear and comprehensible. The nine sections with subsections are cohesive." She also suggested a number of small changes, labeling her revision 6.1. Some of her changes—such as substituting "As valued members of the IIT community" for the opening "Having chosen to associate ourselves with IIT"—were rejected by the exploratory committee (generally, for reasons of style). Most, such as "not splitting a helping verb," were accepted (for example, "might otherwise have" become "might have otherwise"). On February 27, 2007, the code was ready to go before the governing body of the student association—with the faculty council, the president's council, and board of trustees to follow.[17]

The students approved the code in March 2007. The code was to go before the faculty council in the fall, but their schedule and a misunderstanding postponed its vote till February 2008. This is a disappointment. When I agreed to write this article, I expected to be able to describe not only the writing of the code and its ratification but also the first few months of its implementation. That I cannot do so illustrates one of Murphy's many sayings: "Everything takes longer than you think." Happily, it does not illustrate the most famous of Murphy's laws. So far, on the whole, things seem to have gone right.

Once the board of trustees has approved the code, IIT will have to implement it. Among means of implementation now under consideration are (1) including discussion of the code at orientation for new students and new faculty; (2) wide distribution of the code, posting it not only on IIT's Website but on walls around campus; and (3) setting up a body, consisting of members of the IIT community, to answer questions about how to interpret provisions (an "ethics committee"). No doubt, the process of turning a document into a living practice will be even more complicated than preparing the document itself. But describing that process must wait on events yet to come.

Notes

1. Some of this involvement is described in my "Writing a Code of Ethics by E-Mail: Adventures with Software Engineers," *Science Communication*, June 2000, *21*, 392–405; the lessons learned are summarized in my "Eighteen Rules for Writing a Code of Professional Ethics," *Science and Engineering Ethics*, July 2007, *13*, 171–189.

2. For the USC code (2004), see http://www.usc.edu/president/code_of_ethics/ (Oct. 19, 2007). CSEP's librarian did her own search before the meeting and turned up two more. One was for Emory University (a draft posted July 13, 2004, and apparently not yet adopted). It was similar to USC's. The other was for the University of Kentucky (adopted in 2003). Much longer than Emory's or USC's, it began with an interesting list of "core values" that were surprisingly close to Parks's list of "key ideas."

3. See especially my *Profession, Code, and Ethics* (Aldershot, England: Ashgate, 2002).

4. Compare this with the first paragraph of the USC code:

> At the University of Southern California, ethical behavior is predicated on two main pillars: a commitment to discharging our obligations to others in a fair and honest manner, and a commitment to respecting the rights and dignity of all persons. As faculty, staff, students, and trustees, we each bear responsibility not only for the ethics of our own behavior, but also for building USC's stature as an ethical institution.

Apparently, USC did not find this explanation of obligation entirely satisfactory. Near the end of the code, there is another: "Because of the special bonds that bind us together as members of the Trojan Family, we have a familial duty as well as a fiduciary duty to one another." The location of this sentence suggests the poor organization of the code as a whole.

5. See http://www.howard.edu/policy/codeofethics.pdf (Oct. 19, 2007). Howard's code was not the first university code of ethics; nor were Howard's and USC's the only ones extant at that time. They were, it seems, merely the first posted on the Web in a way my method of search brought up. As I prepared this article, I did another search. This one revealed five codes that my earlier search missed: Concordia University (1994); Murdoch University, Australia (1996); Adelphi University (1997); University of Kentucky (2003); and University of Virginia (2004). One more code that the original search might have missed is for Chapman University ("might" because the code is undated). I don't know why I missed the UK code in 2005. The Emory code still seems to be a draft.

6. This, I think, is probably as much a failing in the Howard code as it would be in IIT's. Howard also has architects, engineers, and scientists. In addition, it has practical arts IIT does not have (for example, medicine, divinity, and journalism).

7. Weil's changes were adding to paragraph 1 (academic freedom) the sentence "In this way, we aim to fulfill IIT's mission to advance knowledge through research and scholarship"; and to paragraph 3 (diversity) the sentence "On this basis, we shall seek to build the IIT community." Weil's purpose was to gain authority for these two provisions by connecting them to IIT's Vision and Values Statement. I later objected to both additions because (1) they violated the code's format (one sentence in each paragraph) and (2) they actually added nothing of substance to the code (except perhaps for those who

were familiar enough with IIT's Vision and Values Statement—something to which only administrators seem to pay any attention). Weil saw the sense of these criticisms as soon as they were made. Her additions did not survive into Version 2. No one else noticed either their appearance or disappearance (and I therefore do not quote them below); the additions would probably have not had significant consequence if retained. Still, there is a lesson here. For as long as possible, the actual drafting should be kept in one person's hands. As soon as more than one person begins to do the drafting, the document will begin to lose its distinctive style. Though that moment must come eventually, it should be put off as long as possible, preferably until the code is adopted. This is a point about craft or esthetics of drafting.

8. All quotations in this section come from the official but unpublished minutes of the meeting. I have not given names, to preserve confidentiality, but identified departments to suggest the range of disciplines of those participating. The same is true in succeeding sections describing other focus groups.

9. This is roughly the method Ken Kipnis used successfully to develop a code of ethics for preschool teachers. See his "Toward a Code of Ethics for Pre-School Teachers: The Role of the Ethics Consultant," *International Journal of Applied Philosophy,* Summer 1988, 4, 1–10.

10. It then read:

> Having chosen to associate ourselves with IIT, we—trustees, staff, students, faculty, donors, alumni, and administrators—have become beneficiaries of what our predecessors made and stewards for our successors. For each of us, the benefit derived from association with IIT depends on the conduct of others. If we each do as we should, all associated with IIT will have reason for pride. If even a few fail, we will all have reason for shame; the benefits of association will be less; and we will pass to our successors less than we might otherwise have. This code of ethics is intended to help us all conduct ourselves as we should.

11. This did not bother me. My view of code writing was (and is) that the form of the code should fit the content, not the other way around.

12. Indeed, only two codes (as far as I can tell) do that: the Software Engineering Code of Ethics (www.acm.org/about/se-code, Jan. 8, 2008) and Australian Computer Society Code of Ethics (ethics.iit.edu/codes/coe/aus.computer.soc.code.html, Jan. 8, 2008). Though I helped to draft the SE Code, I had nothing to do with including that explanation in the (very long) preamble.

13. What happened? No one knows for sure, but there seem to be two possibilities. Generally, the trustees like to receive documents a month before a meeting. Version 4.4 may have arrived too late to meet that deadline. Another possibility is that Weil missed the e-mail, supposing it a duplicate of the one that came only a day earlier. Whatever the cause, the effect of using 4.3 rather than 4.4 was long-lasting.

14. The assumption supporting this amendment seems to be that the quality of students is independent of their character—as if, for example, one could be a good student without being an ethical one.

15. The same was also probably true of Hartray and Parks.

16. Comparing Fisher's memory with passages quoted above reveals how untrustworthy memory is, an important reason not only to keep detailed minutes of "interviews" (and focus group meetings) but also of reading them before making claims about their purport.

17. The final version, along with related documents, can be seen at http://ethics.iit.edu/iitcode/index.html (Jan. 8, 2008).

MICHAEL DAVIS is senior fellow at the Center for the Study of Ethics in the Professions and professor of philosophy, Illinois Institute of Technology.

6

Inadequate ethics education has a high price tag in the world of business, burdensome rules and enforcement across global economies and costly consequences for society.

Teaching Ethics in a Business Program

John H. Grant

Societies face continuing challenges in balancing the role of voluntary levels of ethical conduct against those of rules and enforcement. Undergraduate business programs around the world send hundreds of thousands of students into organizations and communities every year, each with his or her own perception of "what's ethical" and "what's legal" under a variety of circumstances.

This article draws on various business situations and research results to illustrate how ethical concepts get connected to standards of practice or conduct during undergraduate (UG) business education. In addition, it offers ways for students to think about the balance between behavior guided by different levels of ethical reasoning versus behavior constrained by various regulations and enforcement mechanisms.

We must remember that ethical reasoning among UG students is influenced by perspectives as diverse as philosophy, economics, religion, professional codes of conduct, and many personal experiences.

Context and Background

Recent years have been filled with numerous highly visible business transactions and relationships that have violated many people's sense of appropriate or ethical business behavior. Such actions have occurred from the top executive suite to the trading floor and production line. As a result, many segments of society feel as though UG business students should be receiving more effective ethics education, while others feel that college-age students are unlikely to alter the ethical reasoning developed during their childhood.

NEW DIRECTIONS FOR HIGHER EDUCATION, no. 142, Summer 2008 © Wiley Periodicals, Inc.
Published online in Wiley InterScience (www.interscience.wiley.com) • DOI: 10.1002/he.304

Businesses and consumers have been seeking honest markets for centuries, and many mechanisms have been designed to try to develop and sustain them. But market failures continue at many organizational levels and throughout much of global commerce. For example, many employees do not fully understand the array of benefits in their compensation packages until they learn they are "not covered" for some medical problem because of imperfections in communication processes. At another level, many big financial institutions have discovered they did not fully understand the economic risks contained in "securitized" residential mortgages they had purchased.

The public accounting profession has had decades of experience involving millions of stakeholders trying to balance the interests of their publicly traded corporate clients against the investors who relied on "certified" financial statements. Weaknesses in this set of relationships led to the demise of Arthur Andersen and to increased regulation of that profession through enactment of Sarbanes-Oxley legislation. The "transaction costs" of such implementation and enforcement serve to highlight the complexities of balancing laws and regulations versus societally accepted business ethics (Hess, 2007). Similar costly complexities arise when the SEC becomes involved in regulating corporate conflicts of interest (Mori, 2007).

In essence, innovations in pursuit of an individual's or organization's advantage in the marketplace will continuously create situations that have not had time to be assessed and addressed by legislative and regulatory processes. Therefore, the importance of ethical principles in the decision-making models of UG business students can scarcely be overstated. Dealing with ethical issues in business across societal levels from the individual to the nation-state can be very challenging. Kaufman (2005) frames the matter this way: "There continues this migration from individual performance as the preferred unit of analysis for performance improvement to one that includes a first consideration of society and external stakeholders; it is responsible, responsive, and ethical to add value to all" (p. 13).

To help address these issues, Giacalone and Thompson (2006) argue for a shift in business schools from an "organizational worldview" (OWV) to a "human worldview" (HWV) as a means of helping students recognize the ethical issues in many aspects of routine commercial operations. Toward that end, Waddock (2007) has suggested that one of the new skills needed by students in the future is ethically based or values-based analysis, so they can more readily recognize the variety of stakeholders affected by particular types of decisions and the future consequences that might result for individuals, organizational reputations, the physical environment, and so forth.

The challenges of achieving and maintaining the "moral high ground" under conditions of intensively competitive markets have been thoroughly addressed by Frank (2003). More recently, Hosmer and Bordelon (2006) and Henderson (2007) have underscored the difficulties in maintaining "ethical markets" when customers and suppliers as well as competitors are very proactive.

In summary, there are many diverse influences on managers' ethical reasoning (Weber and Wasieleski, 2001), so one needs to think about macro systems of social control and the roles various ethical frameworks can play in cultural settings. Next, however, let us consider the nature of UG students' prior experiences and the possible impacts on ethical reasoning.

Student Backgrounds. Although there is a temptation to treat all undergraduate business students as similar, in fact they represent a very diverse subpopulation. Some of them have had little organizational experience beyond their extended family, and others have had years of work experience in a variety of settings.

Recent studies in behavioral economics have found that students can be divided roughly into "self-interested" and "other-interested" categories (Camerer and Fehr, 2006), with the majority in the latter group. At about the same time, research by Rosenau (2006) estimated that only 20–30 percent of people are selfish, chronic free-riders.

Added to these differences are students' varied early courses in such fields as economics, sociology, philosophy, and perhaps religion. Other research has involved the effects of certain common college courses on the strength of self-interest versus cooperative behavior exhibited by students (Frank, Gilovich, and Regan, 2000). Hence, there may be some students who are significantly influenced by undergraduate course content, whether it is taught by business school faculty or their colleagues in another part of the university. If a significant portion of some students' ethical values can be influenced by the curriculum, then the hopes of Mintzberg and his colleagues (Mintzberg, Simons, and Basu, 2002) that there is a need to "move beyond selfishness" in the business world may be realized.

Ethics Education in Undergraduate Business Schools. The Association to Advance Collegiate Schools of Business (AACSB) has become increasingly interested in ethics coverage as part of its accreditation processes in recent years. Shinn (2006) summarized the views of various authorities justifying the AACSB position. At the same time, the Aspen Institute has focused on business education with its "Beyond Pinstripes" initiative (Gentile, 2004).

The literature offers a variety of perspectives regarding ethical decision making in business, as summarized by Loe and colleagues (Loe, Ferrell, and Mansfield, 2000). The dozens of "business ethics centers" across the United States and in other parts of the world attest to the numerous approaches to business ethics education being taken. Weber (2006) has described in considerable detail the efforts being made at his university at both undergraduate and graduate levels.

Many undergraduates find principles-based ethics, involving concepts such as fairness, justice, liberty, honesty, and respect for property rights

(Lawrence and Weber, 2008), to be easier to understand and apply than some virtue-based frameworks. Nonetheless, there is a lot of interest in virtue ethics and their application in the classroom (Battaly, 2006; Copp and Sobel, 2004). Earlier, Lampe's research (1997) led him to the conclusion that teaching business ethics to UGs through philosophical analysis or management cases is not as effective as the use of ethical decision-making models or role modeling.

Although there is a temptation to feel that students who have self-selected into undergraduate business curricula might be somewhat homogeneous in their ethical perspectives, there is reason to be cautious of that conclusion. Significant differences have been found across disciplines as well as between genders and countries of origin (Kidwell, Arzova, and Gegez, 2005). At an aggregate level, if one looks at an "index of ethical business conduct" across dozens of countries, it is easy to recognize the range of behaviors, from the generally high standards in Norway to much lower standards of ethics in many other parts of the world. As UG students begin to think about means of implementing global strategies, their skills in ethical reasoning will almost certainly be thoroughly tested (Singer, 2007).

One framework many students have found useful over the years involves judgment about the types of "social influence mechanisms" that a given society prefers across industries or organizational contexts. As a beginning, one can ask about the extent to which individuals should be allowed to express their personal preferences through choices with more or less ethical content, as illustrated in Figure 6.1. In the case of leisure industries, many people are willing to grant a great deal of individual choice. At the other extreme, participants in the "prison sector" tend to live surrounded by many laws and regulations, with relatively little opportunity for personal choice. Industries such as health care generate lots of debate over appropriate levels of regulation because of the cost of oversight and enforcement versus the expectation of good ethical conduct from the vast majority of health care providers.

Ethics Across Curricular Domains. A basic framework of moral development can be useful for assessing the ethical competencies UG students have acquired. The work of Kohlberg (1981) is among the mostly widely known to business students and helps many of them understand the differences between exclusively self-serving behavior and that which gives consideration to other stakeholders in a decision, even above what local laws or norms might expect (Lawrence and Weber, 2008).

Among the indicators of sophistication in ethical reasoning are the scope of the ethical dilemma being considered and the extent of futurity and precedent being considered. For example, faced with a decision involving clean-up of a chemical spill in a production facility, does a manager think primarily of (1) hiding the evidence with a layer of soil, (2) locating the relevant regulations and following them closely, or (3) recognizing that the evaporating chemicals can pose an immediate fire hazard to employees as

Figure 6.1. Sources and Proportions of Social Control Across Industries

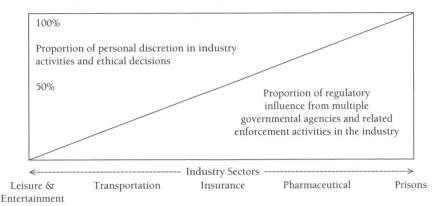

100%

Proportion of personal discretion in industry
activities and ethical decisions

50%

Proportion of regulatory
influence from multiple
governmental agencies and related
enforcement activities in the industry

<----------------------------------- Industry Sectors ------------------------------------>

Leisure &   Transportation   Insurance   Pharmaceutical   Prisons
Entertainment

well as damage to the atmosphere that might adversely affect the broader community, perhaps for years into the future? If time and safety conditions permit, such an event can become a teachable moment for other employees who may face similarly ambiguous conditions at a future date. (The circumstances leading up to an explosion and fire at a BP refinery in the Houston area during March 2005 is one of several similar examples where many decisions over a period of years eventually led to a loss of lives, many human injuries, and major ecological damage—social responsibility measures of organizations that Kaufman, 2000, outlines in his strategic planning model for organizations.)

Choosing or developing "ethical dilemmas" that can easily be edited for changes in technology and geographic location means they can be made to seem currently relevant to students with a variety of backgrounds. Such perceived relevance helps students move beyond ethical abstractions to internalize reasoning processes across disciplines such as those that follow.

Human Resources. Ethical considerations in the domain of interpersonal interactions are among the easiest for most students to recognize. Nonetheless, notions of honesty are stretched frequently, in matters ranging from the authenticity of resumes to discrimination based on personal preferences (Brewer, 2007). Many ethical issues in the HR arena have consequences for family and individual reputations across their communities.

Marketing and Sales. This arena poses significant challenges to students as they seek to determine how much information to disclose to various segments of customers. Issues ranging from the safety of used automobiles to the compatibility of computer system peripherals raise ethical questions that working students or recent graduates must be prepared to address.

Physical Ecosystem. In contrast to the HR and marketing domains, many current business students are not sufficiently aware of some environmental system effects to recognize ethical choices in their daily lives. As students increasingly seek to understand the interactions of the organization within the context of the natural world, they usually begin by thinking about their ethical responsibilities for various types of polluting behavior that might not currently be illegal. Although some business faculty and a few philosophers have been concerned about these issues for decades (Rolston, 1988, 2008), the majority have treated most of the physical ecosystem as an "externality" for purposes of decision making (Arnold and Bustos, 2005; DesJardins, 1999, 2006; Gardiner, 2004).

Production and Logistics. Various operating activities give rise to ethical challenges even before they begin to intersect with marketing or ecosystem considerations. For example, to what extent can a production process be permitted to drift away from control parameters before the product is considered dangerous to employees completing an assembly process, or customers buying the finished product?

Information Systems. At first consideration, many students wonder what ethical issues could arise in designing or implementing information systems, particularly those that are computer-based. However, concern about access to electronic data by different people under various conditions gives rise to many ethical considerations (Moore, 2005; Sheffield and Guo, 2007).

Accounting, Finance, and Legal Services. Much has been written during recent years about "ethical lapses" in the financial systems of major organizations, whether they had independent audits or not (Cheffers and Pakaluk, 2007). Many of the decisions regarding the timing and recognition of noncash transactions can have a major impact on the efficiency of capital markets and which investors benefit or lose from such inefficiencies (Tangpong and Peck, 2007).

Strategic Management. When students begin to analyze the major decisions required of general managers with cross-functional relationships and consequences extending many years into the future, they often become so preoccupied with the technical challenges of integration that they overlook the ethical consequences of the choices expected of them (Grant, 2007; Marcus, 2005; Kaufman, 2000).

Societal Expectations. Undergraduates bring widely differing views of the ethical relationships between firms and their external stakeholders, depending on their family experiences, prior formal education, and personal job contexts. For many UG students, the business-and-society domain is a natural point of connection from traditional business disciplines to other parts of the general education curriculum. Although stakeholders have a variety of relationships to any particular firm or manager (Freeman, Harrison, and Wicks, 2007; Jones, Felps, and Bigley, 2007), the necessity to consider ethical trade-offs is frequently important and often painful. To make principled choices among many stakeholders, there is a need for greater transparency regarding additional performance outcomes, such as

Table 6.1. Ethical Maturity Across Disciplines

Stages of Moral Development*	Natural or Physical Ecosystem	Production and Logistics	Marketing and Sales	Human Resources	Computerized Information Systems	Accounting, Finance, and Legal	Business, Society, and Strategic Management
Mature or sophisticated (human rights, "social contracts")							
Basic (laws, customs, and traditions)							
Primitive or adolescent (emphasis on self-interest)							

*Adapted from Kohlberg (1991).

environmental and social indicators, if managers are to be sufficiently informed to make ethical choices (Grant, forthcoming).

Table 6.1 helps one visualize levels of ethical issues that must be recognized, analyzed, and decided across the disciplines. Faculty members can structure ethical dilemmas that illustrate behavior in each of the numerous cells, or they can develop more complex situations in which students can identify behavior choices that exemplify all three levels of moral or ethical development.

Assessing Ethical Competencies

The process of assessing ethical competencies can take several forms, with many trade-offs governing choices. Decision scenarios are a popular way to give students the opportunity to select the relevant array of stakeholders, the depth of interactions, and the future consequences that would enter a particular decision. When class size and schedule permit, use of debates between sets of students or teams can be a lively means to explore ethical issues. However, assessing open-ended responses or debates can be a very time-consuming and expensive activity, so many schools seek less costly approaches.

Recent efforts to assess the ethical reasoning of UG business students nearing graduation at the University of Northern Colorado led to results suggesting that most students could recognize many forms of unethical business behavior when circumstances were presented in the form of multiple-choice questions. However, such methods do not permit an instructor to assess the reasoning process leading to a particular choice, so many subtleties in a student's analysis could be missed and the resulting stage of moral development misinterpreted. In some settings, administering multiple-choice questions associated with ethical dilemmas can offer a reasonably efficient measure of the moral development achieved by an individual or team of students.

Interactive computer systems are being developed to help students analyze ethical dilemmas in ways that offer the prospect of low variable costs per student, but the fixed investments for development can be substantial. If a few key variables pertaining to technologies, geographical locations, and industries can be easily varied and updated, the prospect of gaining a high level of student interest is enhanced.

As a means of identifying ethical choices at the intersection of various disciplines, a diagram similar to that in Figure 6.2 can be helpful. As long as ethical issues are analyzed exclusively within the confines of a particular discipline, students will miss much of the complexity of the real world. For example, a decision about the recording of a particularly significant sales transaction could easily have ethical implications for accounting, marketing, and human resource units in a firm (systemic implications in business are addressed at length in Stolovitch and Keeps, 1999; ethical implications are

Figure 6.2. Interactions of Ethical Considerations in Commerce

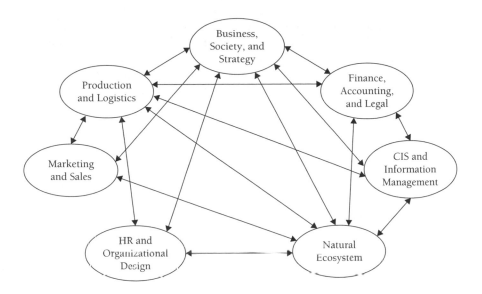

addressed in detail in this systemic manner in Moore, forthcoming). By exposing students to ethical issues along many of the arrows connecting traditional academic disciplines, instructors can be confident their students will be prepared to analyze ethical quandaries in their professional lives.

Looking to the Future

Because of the dynamic contexts of both commercial activity and UG curricula, teaching and assessing ethics material will remain crucial and at the same time challenging during the decades ahead. Nonetheless, like Bardaglio's analysis (2007) of efforts to incorporate sustainability into the UG curriculum, enhancement and refinement of business ethics education probably will involve an extended process of negotiation.

As we reflect on the numerous interrelationships among the ethical dilemmas that will soon face undergraduate students who are about to begin their full-time professional careers, the stakes for society could hardly be higher. Wood and her coauthors (Wood, Logsdon, Lewellyn, and Davenport, 2006) have used the term *global business citizenship* to describe their aspirations for the thought processes and actions of future managers. To achieve such objectives, faculty may need to pursue curriculum integration in a manner similar to Wilson's quest (1999) for "consilience," or the linking of explanations across disciplines.

Conclusions

As we have seen, the treatment of business ethics for undergraduates is extremely important but currently under a great deal of scrutiny. Procedures for assessing the level of ethical reasoning and action extend from the college admissions process through a variety of courses to graduation and beyond. Success or failure in addressing business ethics education will greatly influence society's expenses for rule making and enforcement during the decades ahead. Further investment in ethics education would appear to be the better choice.

References

Arnold, D. G., and Bustos, K. "Business, Ethics and Global Climate Change." *Business and Professional Ethics Journal*, 2005, *24*(1, 2), 103–130.

Bardaglio, P. W. "'A Moment of Grace': Integrating Sustainability into the Undergraduate Curriculum." *Planning for Higher Education*, 2007, *36*(1), 16–22.

Battaly, H. "Teaching Intellectual Virtues: Applying Virtue Epistemology in the Classroom." *Teaching Philosophy*, 2006, *29*(3), 191–222.

Brewer, L. "Is There a Little Bit of Enron in All of Us?" *Journal for Quality and Participation*, 2007, *30*(1), 26–28.

Camerer, C., and Fehr, E. "When Does 'Economic Man' Dominate Social Behavior?" *Science*, 2006, *311*(5757), 47–52.

Cheffers, M., and Pakaluk, M. *Understanding Accounting Ethics* (2nd ed.). Manchaug, Mass: Allen David Press, 2007.

Copp, D., and Sobel, D. "Morality and Virtue: An Assessment of Some Recent Work in Virtue Ethics." *Ethics*, 2004, *114*(3), 514–554.

DesJardins, J. *Environmental Ethics*, Mountain View, Calif.: Mayfield, 1999.

DesJardins, J. *Business, Ethics and the Environment: Imagining a Sustainable Future*. Upper Saddle River, N.J.: Pearson Prentice Hall, 2006.

Frank, R. H. *What Price the Moral High Ground? Ethical Dilemmas in Competitive Environments*. Princeton, N.J.: Princeton University Press, 2003.

Frank, R., Gilovich, T., and Regan, D. "Does Studying Economics Inhibit Cooperation?" In T. Connolly, H. Arkes, and K. Hammond (eds.), *Judgment and Decision Making: An Interdisciplinary Reader* (2nd ed.). Cambridge, UK: Cambridge University Press, 2000.

Freeman, R. E., Harrison, J. S., and Wicks, A. C. *Managing for Stakeholders*. New Haven: Yale University Press, 2007.

Gardiner, S. M. "Ethics and Global Climate Change." *Ethics*, 2004, *114*(3), 555–600.

Gentile, M. "Corporate Governance and Accountability: What Do We Know and What Do We Teach Future Business Leaders?" Presentation at the European Academy of Business in Society's (EABIS) 3rd Annual Colloquium, Vlerick Leuven Gent Management School, Belgium, 2004.

Giacalone, R. A., and Thompson, K. R. "Business Ethics and Social Responsibility: Shifting the Worldview." *Academy of Management Learning and* Education, 2006, *5*(3), 266–277.

Grant, J. H. "Advances and Challenges in Strategic Management." *International Journal of Business*, 2007, *12*(1), 11–31.

Grant, J. H. "Organizational Performance in an Interdependent World." In M. A. Rahim (ed.), *Current Topics in Management*, vol. 13. New Brunswick, N.J.: Transaction, forthcoming.

Henderson, H., with Sethi, S. *Ethical Markets: Growing the Green Economy*. White River Junction, Vt.: Chelsea Green, 2007.

Hess, D. "A Business Ethics Perspective on Sarbanes-Oxley and the Organizational Sentencing Guidelines." *Michigan Law Review*, 2007, *105*, 1781–1818.

Hosmer, L. T., and Bordelon, J. E. "The Morality of Markets." *Business Ethics Quarterly*, 2006, *16*(3), 419–425.

Jones, T. M., Felps, W., and Bigley, G. A. "Ethical Theory and Stakeholder-Related Decisions: The Role of Stakeholder Culture." *Academy of Management Review*, 2007, *32*(1), 137–155.

Kaufman, R. *Mega Planning: Practical Tools for Organizational Success*. Thousand Oaks, Calif.: Sage, 2000.

Kaufman, R. "Defining and Delivering Measurable Value: A Mega Thinking and Planning Primer." *Performance Improvement Quarterly*, 2005, *18*(3), 6–16.

Kidwell, L., Arzova, S. B., and Gegez, A. E. "The Effects of National Culture and Academic Discipline on Responses to Ethical Dilemmas: A Comparison of Students from Turkey and the United States." *Business and Professional Ethics Journal*, 2005, *24*(3), 37–57.

Kohlberg, L. *The Philosophy of Moral Development: Essays on Moral Development*. New York: Harper & Row, 1981.

Lampe, M. "Increasing Effectiveness in Teaching Ethics to Undergraduate Business Students." *Teaching Business Ethics*, 1997, *1*(1), 3–19.

Lawrence, A., and Weber, J. *Business and Society: Stakeholders, Ethics, and Public Policy* (12th ed.). New York: McGraw-Hill Irwin, 2008.

Loe, T., Ferrell, L., and Mansfield, P. "A Review of Empirical Studies Assessing Ethical Decision Making in Business." *Journal of Business Ethics*, 2000, *25*(3), 185–204.

Marcus, A. *Management Strategy: Sustaining Competitive Advantage*. New York: McGraw Hill/Irwin, 2005.

Mintzberg, H., Simons, R., and Basu, K. "Beyond Selfishness." *MIT Sloan Management Review*, 2002, *44*(1), 67–74.

Moore, S. L. "The Social Impact of a Profession: An Analysis of Factors Influencing Ethics and the Teaching of Social Responsibility in Educational Technology Programs." Unpublished doctoral dissertation, Department of Educational Technology, University of Northern Colorado, 2005.

Moore, S. L. *Ethics by Design: A New Definition of Performance Standards and Performance Accountability*. HRD Press, forthcoming.

Mori, M. "A Proposal to Revise the SEC Instructions for Reporting Waivers of Corporate Codes of Ethics for Conflicts of Interest." *Yale Journal on Regulation*, 2007, *24*(2), 293–312.

Rolston III, H. *Environmental Ethics*. Philadelphia: Temple University Press, 1988.

Rolston III, H. "Ethical Dimensions of Global Warming." Presentation at Focus the Nation conference, Ft. Collins, Colo., Jan., 30, 2008.

Rosenau, P. "Is Economic Theory Wrong About Human Nature?" *Journal of Economic and Social Policy*, 2006, *10*(2), 61–77.

Sheffield, J., and Guo, Z. "Ethical Inquiry in Knowledge Management." In R. Attwater and J. Merson (eds.), *Sustaining Our Social and Natural Capital*. Mansfield, Mass.: ISCE, 2007.

Shinn, S. "On Course with Ethics." *BizEd*, Sept./Oct. 2006, 22–29.

Singer, A. E. "Global Strategy & Ethics." *Business Ethics Quarterly*, 2007, *17*(2), 341–363.

Stolovitch, H., and Keeps, E. (eds.). *Handbook of Human Performance Technology* (2nd ed.). San Francisco: Jossey-Bass, 1999.

Tangpong, C., and Peck, J. "Shareholder Value Ideology, Reciprocity and Decision Making in Moral Dilemmas." *Journal of Managerial Issues*, 2007, *19*(3), 379–396.

Waddock, S. "Leadership Integrity in a Fractured Knowledge World." *Academy of Management Learning and Education*, 2007, *6*(4), 543–557.

Weber, J. "Implementing an Organizational Ethics Program in an Academic Environment: The Challenges and Opportunities for the Duquesne University Schools of Business." *Journal of Business Ethics*, 2006, *65*(1), 23–42.

Weber, J., and Wasieleski, D. "Investigating Influences on Managers' Morals." *Business and Society*, 2001, *40*, 79–111.

Wilson, E. O. *Consilience: The Unity of Knowledge*. New York: Vintage Books, 1999.

Wood, D. J., Logsdon, J. M., Lewellyn, P. G., and Davenport, K. *Global Business Citizenship: A Transformative Framework for Ethics and Sustainable Capitalism*. Armonk, New York: M. E. Sharpe, 2006.

Additional Resources

Association to Advance Collegiate Schools of Business
   www.aacsb.edu/resource_centers/EthicsEdu/
Association of American Colleges and Universities
   www.aacu.org/issues/assessment/ethical_behavior.cfm
Business as an Agent of World Benefit
   www.BAWBGlobalForum.org
Center for Ethical Deliberation
   www.mcb.unco.edu/ced.index.cfm
Council of Ethical Organizations
   www.corporateethics.com
Ethics Resource Center
   www.ethics.org
Framework for Universal Principles of Ethics by L. Colero
   www.ethics.ubc.ca/papers/invited/colero.html
International Society for Environmental Ethics
   www.cep.unt.edu/ISEE.html
Kenan Institute for Ethics
   http://kenan.ethics.duke.edu/prog_details.asp?actID=44
Self-Assessment and Improvement Process (SAIP)
   www.stthomas.edu/cob/about/ethics/resources/saip.html
Society for Business Ethics
   www.societyforbusinessethics.org
Zicklin Center for Business Ethics Research
   www.zicklincenter.org/Research.htm

JOHN H. GRANT *is a visiting professor of management at the Monfort College of Business, University of Northern Colorado.*

7

An example of how one faculty member in instructional technology developed a course integrating ethics into her program's curriculum.

Classroom Strategies for Teaching Ethics

Sharon Smaldino

Tackling a course in professional standards and ethical practice in instructional technology is a daunting task indeed. Why bother with such a course? What is the value of such a topic within an already crowded program of study? Just because it is a standard dictated by the new state license requirements, is it necessary to isolate the topic as a stand-alone course? Is there an existing course within the university setting that might serve to meet this need? Such issues were the impetus behind the development of just such a course for a master's-level program of study.

Many questions exist regarding this topic, with few direct answers. In examining the logistics of the new program of study for technology specialist, a designation recently implemented by the state of Illinois, the requirements for the specialist's endorsement became the standard for the course design. The rationale for the state's decisions to add topics such as standards and ethics was not clearly articulated; however, the requirements were defined by the curriculum developers as existing beyond the mere need for saying standards and ethics discussions are present in the program of study for those seeking the endorsement.

The criteria, established externally by the state, present themselves as a conundrum that often faces faculty with regard to states' regulations being aligned with integrating technology into the curriculum. It's a slippery slope and akin to one of my favorite book titles about technology, *Nailing Jelly to a Tree*. Where to begin and what to do? The developmental process and the implementation of a course specific to this topic of study have led to many insights as to the value of such an endeavor.

NEW DIRECTIONS FOR HIGHER EDUCATION, no. 142, Summer 2008 © Wiley Periodicals, Inc.
Published online in Wiley InterScience (www.interscience.wiley.com) • DOI: 10.1002/he.305

Purpose for the Course

The recently identified Illinois state standards associated with the newly designated technology specialist (TS) endorsement required the graduate faculty to
explore the issues associated with addressing those standards and ensuring curriculum alignment. The entire list of endorsement standards includes a balance
between knowledge and skills that can be used as a professional guide for
schools to effectively integrate technology in support of student learning. Such
a school employee balances the need for specific skills to assist technology-
supported teachers with the educational benefits realized from bringing technology into the learning setting for children. The dual-focused idea is a
common one among many professionals; it articulates the need to have an educator who is skilled in the hardware and software issues but also knowledge-
able in implementation of effective technology integration into learning. There
has been a need expressed by professionals for this type of balance for many
years (Smaldino, Lowther, and Russell, 2008), and the development of an
endorsement related to a teaching certificate encourages educators to develop
such proficiencies. As technology becomes a part of most classrooms, it
becomes necessary for school district administrators to identify the roles such
a technology person will serve within the schools and to specify the required
performance skills. Gone are the days where just saying you "can do it" is sufficient. We need to design a more proficient way of identifying individuals who
can serve the learning interests of students by using technology tools.

Examining the state standards relative to professional standards and
ethical practice, one finds a number of indicators offering direction on
where to begin:

- Identifies, designs, and practices strategies for using learning technologies with diverse populations such as at-risk students and students with
  disabilities
- Identifies professional organizations, groups, and resources that support
  the field of educational computing and technology
- Designs and practices methods for teaching social, ethical, and legal issues
  surrounding the responsible use of technology
- Identifies research related to human and equity issues concerning the use
  of computers and related technologies in education
- Develops and implements ethical and legal procedures for maintaining
  software libraries
- Identifies and classifies assistive technology for students and teachers with
  special needs and locates sources to assist in their procurement and
  implementation [Illinois State Board of Education, Technology Specialist
  Matrix]

This list of standards related to practice represents only a small fraction of
the types of ethical issues encountered daily by instructional technology

professionals (Spinello, 2003). Clearly the state's proposed list of standards is highly focused and constrained to the view of a PK–12 educator. But most instructional technology programs do not merely serve the PK–12 world. Many of them serve a larger body of professional endeavors, including corporate and higher education areas. The logical next question then becomes: Can a course that addresses these specific areas meet the needs of these other professionals?

Inquiry into What Was Available. As the discussion among the faculty ensued, it became apparent that two issues had to be addressed. The first was, Can this standard for the technology specialist endorsement be met by taking a course within another university department? The second: Does the content appear in a variety of courses within the instructional technology program of study being designed? These are two critical issues to address when designing a program of study that is connected to a state license endorsement. The faculty realized that not every topic or standard required a stand-alone course. As with other programs, many topics are successfully integrated into the existing curriculum across a set of courses.

Tackling the first question, can this be met by another course somewhere outside of the department structure? A quick scan of available courses across the university indicated a high degree of specificity among the courses related to fields of study such as computer science, business, and information management. But because of the nature of the targeted audience for these courses, the learning objectives did not cover issues appropriate to the PK–12 technology specialist professional. Also, some of the included topics appeared to be irrelevant when aligning with the specified standards.

A further review of cross-campus general philosophy courses in ethics failed to identify issues associated with professional standards. Not a daunting issue in itself, but in further examining the types of issues addressed in this category of course, topics were clearly outside the realm of the PK–12 educator, and even though perhaps interesting, they were not relevant to helping those seeking this endorsement in achieving their goals. Many courses of this type outside the College of Education (COE) deal with medical or legal ethical issues that, again, may not be relevant to the educator seeking the TS endorsement. This finding supported the concern of the instructional technology graduate faculty fact-finding team for bringing relevancy, as an important component, into the selection of how to address the elements articulated within the standards.

The second question, examining the existing curriculum within the COE's instructional technology program content, was the next logical step. Although snippets of issues are raised in existing courses, the concern for an expanded inclusion of in-depth discussions and activities was identified. How can faculty ensure that the professional who is awarded this endorsement has the knowledge and comprehension of these issues? Does the manner in which the related topic of standards and professional practice are taught make enough of an impact over the duration of the program of study?

Again, recognizing that many faculty members reinforce the concepts of standards and practice within their own courses, the nature of the state standards are such that the topic itself had to be addressed and discussed in depth with specified guidelines. Thus the decision was made to create a separate full-semester course designed to investigate the topics of standards and practice with a focus on each element associated with each area of concern. This graduate-faculty decision initiated a search for existing instructional technology program models that demonstrated effective practice addressing the topic of ethics and standards.

Identifying Curriculum. Following the inquiry into what was already available at the university level, it became apparent that there are many nuances surrounding the topic of ethical practice that should be considered. With the decision to address this topic as an individual course, the apparent constraint to determine ways to keep this manageable within a semester-long course became tantamount to holding a tiger by the tail. After examining the standards and expectations of the state and looking at the levels of depth required for a clear understanding of the issues, we saw that there was a distinct need to look specifically at the instructional technology field's efforts in this critical area.

The first step was to look at relevant professional organizations and their standards and expectations concerning the knowledge of standards and engagement in ethical practice. In examining many organizations' standards, we determined that many exist as guidelines or as steps to follow within the particular instructional technology area identified. However, only one organization had a committee structure charged with the task of identifying and addressing professional standards and ethical practice (AECT Professional Ethics Committee, 2007).

Further, the faculty committee believed it was important to consider the background and experience of those students who would enroll in this course. What experiences and knowledge do they bring with them? What scope of the issues have they already addressed in other courses or discussions? Following accepted instructional design principles (Dick, Carey, and Carey, 2004; Smith and Ragan, 2004), identification of the intended learners was one of many subsequent steps that had to be done toward developing a specific course.

The decision to identify Instructional Technology programs where the topic of standards and ethical practice was addressed was considered necessary in order to gain insight and understanding of how the topic could be managed. This led to an Internet search of courses or ideas related to the topic to determine the best approach to guide the master's-level students seeking the TS endorsement. In searching for what was already available, it became apparent that the field of instructional technology did not abound with courses of this nature. Where they did exist, the content did not serve well in preparing students to meet the specified state endorsement standards in the area of standards and practice. There appeared to be a current mix of surface-level and limited-scope topics available. The need for a single course that addressed standards and practice was clearly one that had not been completely encountered prior to this endeavor.

Issues to Be Addressed. The one area that has focused on ethical considerations is the field of computer science. Moor (cited in Tavani, 2007) suggests in a book on ethics and technology written for computer science students that the "computer/information revolution has changed our lives and has brought with it significant ethical, social, and professional issues" (p. xxvii). He further suggests that constant changes within the world of technology continue to challenge professionals in their daily practice. Moor further contends that the expectations and experiences we have do not necessarily prepare us for each new shift in technology. Moor recommends that we continuously explore and address topics related to standards and ethical practice that are critical to all professionals.

Another computer science professor, Spinello (2003), identifies the growth of the Web and the Internet as factors that have influenced the need for study in areas of privacy, free speech, and intellectual property. His instructional approach of using case studies related to information technology ethical issues attempts to have professionals "reflect on the vexing ethical dilemmas and problems that are emerging in the information age" (p. xii). He further contends that the *rules* rapidly change and that problems encountered along the way must be examined. Spinello suggests that professionals need to build an understanding of ethical issues as they exist and a "cogent action plan within the bounds of ethical probity and social acceptability" (p. xiii).

The Illinois standards suggest that there are more areas of concern than privacy, free speech, and intellectual property (Illinois State Board of Education, 2007). An expanded view includes such topics as equity and accessibility. Security and safety, embracing those issues related to health and welfare, are also critical to include in a program of study. Finally, although Tavani and Spinello do advise the need for professionalism, they do not necessarily focus on the study of specific professional standards in the area of technology and learning for PK–12 students or even instructors.

Approach to Design

Framework for Design and Content Selection Issues. Because the indicators for the standards related to professional issues are clearly enunciated by the state of Illinois, the decision to use those standards as a guide served as the frame around which a course on ethics and standards was organized. Further, on the basis of experience with classroom instruction, assumptions were identified regarding the background knowledge of students who would enroll in this course. One major assumption was that although these students may have a rudimentary knowledge of copyright issues, especially in the area of fair use, they might not have the expansive knowledge necessary to be a school leader versed in the array of standards and practices identified by the state.

Other considerations were also framed by the standards. Many of the educators who were identified for this particular master's program had an elementary or secondary education background. The graduate students' expressed limited knowledge of health and safety issues, as well as little or no understanding of issues associated with accessibility. The need to guide teachers in understanding these factors as a part of the teachers' role as technology specialists in the schools is critical. Finally, policy plus social and ethical issues were elements that had to be confronted explicitly. The course developer believed these were factors that needed to be brought into the discussions throughout the semester.

Many of the current textbooks and resource tools in this area of standards and ethics reside in the fields of computer science and information management. Even within those fields of study, there are issues regarding the instructional approach to adopt. Tavani (2007) proposed that the study of applied ethics, rather than theoretical ethics, was the crux in understanding the role of the professional in the field of computer science. This suggested approach does not appear to be content-dependent. One could argue that Tavani's point fits well into any aspect of a professional study of ethical practice, including the PK–12 technology integration field. Examining issues within the designated context requires understanding how to address these issues with an ethical view. Gotterbarn (1995) suggested that the study of ethics for technology-related fields links to professional responsibility, rather than larger moral implications of technology applications. His focus on individual responsibility argues that it is not so critical to address the moral and ethical issues within the study as it is the approaches one takes to identify and resolve the problems encountered. Johnson (2000) suggests that much of what professionals encounter in their daily practice is part of what she terms *ordinary ethics*. She proposes that the need for such study will decline and eventually disappear from most curricula. Johnson contends that as educators become better able to integrate technology into their teaching, they will no longer need to overtly address the ethical issues as they assume an ethical posture in their practice.

These discussions among the computer science professionals are valuable to examine, but they do not present an easy solution to the problem of addressing the state's identified criteria for professionalism in the context of standards and practice in the PK–12 arena.

Sequencing of Topics.   Once it was decided that the newly developed course would focus on professional standards and ethical practice, the manner in which to address the topics became the next phase in the design process. The design methodology was to use a logical framework that addressed the study of topics from a broad perspective to a narrow one. This approach served as the guide to decisions related to the selected topic sequence.

At some point in their educational history, most educators have had some experience with exploring morals, values, and ethics. But for many, these issues were embedded within a general course of study as part of a general education component of their undergraduate program. In exploring available resources and considering the standards that were to be addressed, the researchers made the decision to include a brief review of ethical frameworks to "help us assess behavior in complex situations where critical ethical analysis is necessary" (Spinello, 2003, p. 1).

A compounding factor in determining the need for including an ethical framework is the rapid growth and expansion of technology with every new iteration of technology advancement. Many educators have not explored the issues of values and ethics within the framework of current-day technology advances. Moor (cited in Tavani, 2007) suggests that the growth of technology devices will necessitate studying present applications and preparing us to deal with an *uncertain future* in computing power. He considers a study of ethics and technology critical for the professionals' role within the cyberworld of tomorrow.

The course design started with exploration of the definitions of morals, values, and ethics. This task gave the students in the program a beginning framework with which to examine the issues raised related to integrating technology applications in schools. The Illinois endorsement standards served to focus topics for the sequencing decisions. A logic model approach was beneficial in diagramming and examining the identified outcomes with the best approaches to meeting the standards, and thus ensuring that students in the program would be eligible for the endorsement on completion of their study. By using a logic model diagram, students could make the links to the components of the learning outcomes reflect the sequence of content necessary to be effective (see Table 7.1).

The instructional methodology flowed from development of a framework for understanding ethical practice. With this framework in mind, the specific topics of technology application in PK–12 education could be explored, recognizing that there were no simple answers to some of the issues raised.

Strategies of Teaching. Though there were many instructional approaches that could be applied, the suggestion by Spinello (2003) of a case study slant seemed to fit best into the nature of this course plan. The instructional designer believed the students could begin to apply their newly formed ethical frameworks to solving problems presented by exploring the topics within a given context. The cases selected were designed around the broad topics identified within the standards for the state endorsement. The standards-focused design is intended so that, on successful completion of this course of study, those seeking the endorsement will have met the specified standards.

Once this approach was determined to be most efficient in terms of the topics raised, it was time to consider how best to present the topics to the students. The approach to using case study followed a pattern of an

Table 7.1. Sample Logic Model for Course Planning

Standards	Resources and Inputs	Activities	Outputs and Products
The state or professional standards	What resources are needed?	Activities to guide learning	Student outputs and products as evidence
Identifies, designs, and practices strategies for using learning technologies with diverse populations such as at-risk students and students with disabilities	Reading materials, library resources, Web-based resources	Prompts for discussions, literature review paper, case study	Online discussion responses to prompts, possible literature review paper topic, development of resolution to case study
Identifies professional organizations, groups, and resources that support the field of educational computing and technology	Reading materials, library resources, Web-based resources	Prompts for discussions, case study	Online discussion responses to prompts, development of resolution to case study
Designs and practices methods for teaching social, ethical, and legal issues surrounding responsible use of technology	Reading materials, library resources, Web-based resources	Prompts for discussions, literature review paper, case study, novel review	Online discussion responses to prompts, possible literature review paper topic, development of resolution to case study, novel review and discussion
Identify and apply copyright and fair use guidelines within practice	Reading materials, library resources, Web-based resources	Prompts for discussions, literature review paper, case study	Online discussion responses to prompts, possible literature review paper topic, development of resolution to case study

initial investigation of the situation, research of the issues, classroom debate, and finally a class consensus statement regarding a solution.

A balance of collaborative and individual work was considered to be the best approach to guiding students in their course of study. It is widely known among faculty that many graduate students do not enjoy working in groups; they feel that their success is lost within any group limitations. It was a conscious decision to engage the students in the study of the cases as groups, thus capitalizing on the combination of many ideas to present solutions to the problems.

The individual work was carefully organized around having students use their newly gained knowledge to enhance collective decisions. Thus, in addition to the case studies, specific topics were identified as the focus for large group discussions. For example, the issue of equity of technology access was a general large group discussion, with each individual expected to expand the discussion by providing explicit examples and designated resources to support her or his arguments. Instructor probing and other facilitation techniques were additional means to move discussion beyond the surface level.

Because the course is graduate-level, the expectations for students included a degree of rigor such that they demonstrate their abilities to synthesize, evaluate, and articulate their comprehension of the topics. The need to offer sufficient instructional experiences within the course dictated a balance among the amount of time for discussion, the manner of assessment, and the degree of rigor.

A blended-course approach of online and face-to-face delivery was initially examined. The use of an online course management tool offered an opportunity to develop forums in which students could engage in asynchronous discussions of the case studies and the assigned topics for general discussion. The face-to-face class time was devoted to developing a discussion framework with the focus on morals, values, and ethics, and also to developing collaborative group strategies. Students were expected to attend the face-to-face meetings in order to share and learn from each other in much the same way they were expected to participate in the online discussions.

The case study topics for the course included:

- Free expression in cyberspace
- Intellectual property issues
- Privacy and information access
- Liability, reliability, and safety

The general discussion topics for the course included:

- Professional standards and professional organizations
- Policy, procedures, and practice
- Media representation of technology
- Equity of access and health and personal safety

A final task, a literature review paper, was assigned to each student on a topic of interest that was to be investigated in depth. Because of the limited experience many of the students had with writing literature review papers, the instructor supplied them with feedback on a draft of the final paper at the midpoint of the course. This feedback gave students information on how their approach to the final paper was progressing.

As an activity to offer students a break from their intense paper draft preparation (and giving the instructor some time to read and respond to each student's paper), another type of assignment was included: reading a science fiction novel in which technology was used in a unique (and often dangerous) manner. Because students in a traditional graduate program range in age and experience, a variety of book choices were supplied—classical, modern, and adolescent literature. Students were not restricted to this list but were encouraged to recognize that their selection had to include technology as a critical component to the story line. The reading assignment was a natural segue into discussion of how the media represents technology in everyday life and in schools in particular. This in turn led into subsequent class discussion about equity and safety and health issues.

Analysis of Results and Feedback

In developing a new course, one must determine what works and what can be improved. Thus a critical component of this course strategy was to identify a number of ways in which to collect information about the instructional strategies employed and the types of tasks assigned. Both formative and summative assessment and evaluation tools were built into the course design.

In a blended or completely online course, there is often the complaint that the work level is far too intense compared to campus-based face-to-face classes. These student comments supported the designer's belief that she should learn from the students. Of particular interest was determining which of the specific approaches employed worked well and which required changes. The data used for making decisions about future iterations of this course came from actual student assignment grade data and from the reflection statements they offered periodically throughout the semester. Students completed four reflections over the course of the semester. The latter was also an assigned task, but the instructor made certain that the students felt comfortable in sharing information about their impressions of the content and the structure of the course. Students were given stems to use as a guide to writing the opening sentences in their reflections, many of which were developed to allow students to express negative as well as positive statements about their impression of the design and effectiveness of the course. These stems included phrases such as "I never knew that . . .," "I never realized that . . .," "I never thought of . . .," "I never expected . . .," "I appreciate that . . .," "I need to learn . . .," "I have a better understanding of . . .," "Implications for my learning. . . ."

Students were not limited to these stems; nor were they limited in their creativity to meet this assignment. For the most part, they used these stems as a guide for writing their reflections. The instructor used these comments as her cue to making improvements in the course.

Student Data from Coursework. Generally, students completed assignments at the expected level of accomplishment for graduate work. In many cases, on receiving feedback about an assignment students immediately intensified their work ethic to produce even higher quality work for subsequent assignments. On the basis of the grading used for the course, the majority of the students met or exceeded expectations in their group and individual assignments.

Student Reflections as a Guide. Student reflections certainly presented another view of the course beyond coursework grades. In an initial reflection, one student summed up what many felt was a concern, the need for a whole course on this topic:

> When I first realized that I was required to take an Ethics class for this Master's Degree in Instructional Technology, I wondered how on earth an Ethics class could possibly fill sixteen weeks. It seemed to me that it would be a subject that could easily be suitable for half the semester, but a stretch to fill the entire semester. I also wondered why this course was required since we have discussed ethics cases in a few of the classes that I have already taken. Now that I have seen the amount of work required by this class, I can understand the sixteen weeks needed.

Another student, in an initial reflection, stated that the topic was relevant to her daily professional responsibilities:

> I felt it was important to acquire a good foundation in the area of professional responsibility and ethics. This is what initially attracted me to this course. As a librarian at a middle school, topics such as the responsible use of technology, copyright, digital divide and ethical practices often arise in my position. Working with a staff of nearly seventy-five, it is important that I stay abreast of current trends in technology but also what is fair and ethical.

As the semester progressed, subsequent reflections permitted even greater understanding of the students' interests and intrinsic motivation for a course devoted to examining standards and ethical practice. One student, who was not a PK–12 educator, noted:

> Technology has become such an integral part of society that it seems to be becoming unmanageable. The moment there is a solution to a problem or a law developed a new technology is on the horizon to present additional issues. Technology has so many benefits but it also brings a plethora of problems that need to be considered.

A student who had little to say earlier in the semester summed up his perceptions of the topics of study within the course by stating:

NEW DIRECTIONS FOR HIGHER EDUCATION • DOI: 10.1002/he

> I have definitely developed a better appreciation for the potential for controversy when dealing with technology. It seems like it should be easy for Congress to create laws to govern the internet and address issues like data privacy, identity theft, and others. However the pace of the development of new technologies makes it extremely difficult to legislate for current and future needs.

Students concurred that the topics selected were based on those very things the state identified as essential for the technology specialist in the schools. Student realizations included the observation that a person would have to be familiar not only with the rules and regulations of the school district but also with more general legal aspects. When working with other professionals, the technology specialist must have the ability to recognize the scope of the issue and help educators meet the challenge professionally, ethically, and legally.

When it came to giving feedback on the actual design of the course, several students voiced their opinions. One older international student stated:

> This method of sharing summary on Discussion Board helped the student . . . [and] is yet another technique of learning and sharing. The approach taken in case studies to summarize and come up with key ideas with possible solution and a question to challenge the student is an interesting and new concept to me. It will surely be a fun to see comments from the peers in the next week on case studies. I enjoy this course and every week I am learning something new. I am certainly happy to take this course and I am looking forward to learn more in the coming weeks.

Not all students found the organization of the course facilitated the kind of learning experience they expected. Several also thought that using the online approach for facilitating the discussions made it difficult to engage in meaningful dialogue. Several students made statements similar to this one:

> To be honest I don't feel much real discussion was possible with the sheer number of posts and replies we each had to complete. I can't say I really remember half of what I responded. And I can't remember much of what others added. With the limited amount of time I've had these past weeks, and the amount of time it took to read the case study threads, I didn't have near the time I had planned to use working on my rough draft for the literature review paper.

But overall, students were very satisfied with the type of experience and the knowledge they gained within the context of a course that explored technology standards and ethics. One student summed up what many also stated:

> Hard to believe it's May already! I think back to the first class in Naperville in very, very cold January. After sitting through the first fifteen minutes, my

gut reaction was to drop this class. The work seemed staggering. I work full-time and although my children are young adults, I do have some other family responsibilities that require a good deal of my time. Could I do this? Do I want to do this? Am I selling myself short if I quit before I even get started not to mention that I have never dropped a college class before in my life and I am not even sure how to go about doing that—another problem. So, I persevered. I trudged through a myriad of new situations—online discussions, online postings, papers, some tough reading assignments and deadlines. I am satisfied to say that I am glad I hung in there. I enjoyed the challenge and gained some great insight into some difficult topics.

Conclusions and Recommendations

An integral part of designing and implementing a course is to evaluate the impact of the course in regard to the intended outcomes. One measure of success is that a number of students who completed their program of study have been granted state endorsement as a technology specialist. There are many others who are nearing completion of their program, and more data will be available as to student success in terms of achieving the goal of a state license.

Lessons Learned. In terms of the success of a single course in standards and ethical practice, most students concluded at the end of the sixteen weeks that they benefited in having taken the course. As part of the evaluation of the course, students identified specific areas where they felt there needed to be improvement. Their feedback on these specifics was gathered in a face-to-face final meeting night at the end of the four-month class.

Students expressed the need for longer discussion opportunities. Several expressed concern that the online discussion board option failed to supply the depth they would have liked. Several mentioned that their group discussions for the case study presentations attained the level of quality engagement they had hoped for in the asynchronous discussions of the general topics with the whole class.

Another area that students suggested was in the type of cases assigned to analyze and summarize. Some PK–12 educators felt that Spinello's case studies (2003) were not specific to their particular situations. The instructor agreed with this observation regarding the relevance of some of the topics under discussion. Nonetheless, many of these PK–12 educators did suggest it was helpful to see that other technology professionals were struggling with issues that were aligned with some of those within the field of instructional technology. The students' general perception was that the selected cases should be more in line with their area of interest: the application of technology in learning.

What was most surprising for the instructor was that the major task, the literature review paper, was not identified as being an unrealistic expectation. Earlier in the semester, there seemed to be general concern about such a requirement. After completion of the task, however, students voiced that they liked doing the paper and learned much from their inquiries into a chosen specific topic. The general student feedback suggested that students post their paper, or at least an executive summary or abstract, for the rest of the class. This suggestion may have grown from interest in what classmates shared during the discussions conducted during the semester, which related in some ways to the insights they were gleaning from their paper inquiries. Students enjoyed learning from each other and being guided to new resources.

Although it may seem daunting that a whole semester be devoted to the study of professional standards and ethical practice, a well-organized and structured course can meet student needs in understanding and engaging in ethical practice in their professional lives. This course demonstrates that a variety of activities and the relevance of the topics should match the students' interests and preparation for their professional future. The students' ability to effectively master the topics through their assignments and their exchange of ideas indicated that they were able to grasp the need for an intensive study of the topics.

Where to Venture Next.   Given the nature of professional technology standards and issues, this course will continue to evolve. There are a number of options to explore for the future. Because students felt the discussions were of value, albeit perhaps not as interactive as they preferred thanks to the asynchronous nature of the course design and heavy use of the course management tool, alternative approaches are being explored. One suggestion is to have group discussions on the topics and share summaries of the separate group discussions with the rest of the class.

Another idea is to use an alternative to the asynchronous course management tool. Why not take a course like this into Second Life or another virtual environment? The dynamics of bringing together the members of the class with other audiences could create the depth and breadth that several students felt were missing from an online approach. This is an approach being explored currently. Small and large group activities have been organized to follow a pattern similar to the previous version of the course, but with the use of synchronous dimension as the frame for the discussions.

In Conclusion.   It has been an interesting endeavor to explore this topic and design a course that addressed an area of inquiry students may not have recognized as being important within their study. The topic of ethics is broader and deeper than most professionals recognize. By delving into this topic, I learned much about the issues of standards and ethical practice. In the process I enjoyed the opportunity to explore interesting approaches to addressing what might have been considered an extraneous subject in the instructional technology field of study.

References

Association for Educational Communication and Technology (AECT) Professional Ethics Committee. Retrieved Sept. 21, 2007, from http://www.aect.org/about/div_.asp? DivisionID = 28.

Dick, W., Carey, L., and Carey, J. *The Systematic Design of Instruction* (6th ed.). New York: Allyn and Bacon, 2004.

Gotterbarn, D. "Computer Ethics: Responsibility Regained." In D. G. Johnson and H. Nissenbaum (eds.), *Computing, Ethics, and Social Values.* Upper Saddle River, N.J.: Prentice Hall, 1995.

Illinois State Board of Education. Retrieved Sept. 21, 2007, from http://www.isbe.net/ profprep/pcstandardrules.htm.

Johnson, D. "The Future of Computer Ethics." In G. Collste (ed.), *Ethics in the Age of Information Technology.* Linkoping, Sweden: Centre for Applied Ethics, 2000.

Smaldino, S., Lowther, D., and Russell, J. *Instructional Technology and Media for Learning* (9th ed.). Upper Saddle River, N.J.: Prentice Hall, 2008.

Smith, P., and Ragan, T. *Instructional Design* (3rd ed). Hoboken, N.J.: Wiley, 2004.

Spinello, R. A. *Case Studies in Information Technology Ethics* (2nd ed.). Upper Saddle River, N.J.: Prentice Hall, 2003.

Tavani, H. T. *Ethics and Technology: Ethical Issues in an Age of Information and Communication Technology* (2nd ed.). Hoboken, N.J.: Wiley, 2007.

SHARON SMALDINO holds the LD & Ruth G. Morgridge Endowed Chair for Teacher Education at Northern Illinois University; she can be reached at ssmaldino@niu.edu.

NEW DIRECTIONS FOR HIGHER EDUCATION • DOI: 10.1002/he

8

Universities and athletic departments have the ethical responsibility to offer athletes a meaningful educational experience.

The Institution's Obligations to Athletes

Linda A. Sharp, Holly K. Sheilley

This entire article could consist of nothing more than diatribe after diatribe of those who assail the current state of college sports. Commentators discuss the evidence showing that "college sports are rife with corruption" (Benford, 2007, p. 1). It is often noted that reform efforts, ranging from the Carnegie Foundation's 1929 report on *American College Athletics* (Savage, 1929) to the three generations of the Knight Commission reports (1991, 1993, 2001), have essentially failed in efforts to tame the beast of commercialization or reduce the degree to which Division I athletics has become "edutainment" (Benford, 2007; Sperber, 2000; Zimbalist, 1999; Shulman and Bowen, 2001), a reference to the increasing encroachment of the entertainment model upon the academic values of educational institutions.

Many commentators have noted how the increasing commercialization of college sports has made it even more difficult for universities to reconcile the gap between college sports and the fundamental mission of higher education. Allen Sack (2001, p. B7), a well-known commentator on collegiate sport, stated: "Longer seasons, significantly lower admission standards for athletes, and the growing power of coaches over all aspects of an athlete's life are just a few of the changes spawned by the unprecedented commercialism that has invaded athletics departments." Numerous books have addressed the basic incompatibility of big-time college athletics and educational primacy (Sack and Staurowsky, 1998; Sperber, 2000; Shulman and Bowen, 2001; Duderstadt, 2000; Zimbalist, 1999). Eitzen (2000, p. 30) has captured the essence of the concerns: "Not only do typical athletes in big-time sports enter at an academic disadvantage, they often encounter a diluted educational experience while attending their schools. Coaches, under the

Published online in Wiley InterScience (www.interscience.wiley.com) • DOI: 10.1002/he.306

103

intense pressure to win, tend to diminish the student side of their athletes by counseling them to take easy courses, choose easy majors, and enroll in courses given by faculty members friendly to the athletic department."

In sum, many commentators believe that the current commercial structure of big-time college sports is essentially incompatible with education (Eitzen, 2000; Sack, 2001).

In contrast to these sentiments, the NCAA and its member institutions prioritize the importance of the educational process and academic success, explicitly acknowledging that the academic interests of student and college athlete are indistinguishable. For example, Myles Brand, president of the NCAA, spoke to this issue: "Since the participants in college sports are students—individuals whose first business is acquiring an education—their academic success is of central importance" (Brand, 2006).

The 2007–08 NCAA Division I Manual (§§2.2 and 2.4) also emphasizes educational primacy:

> Intercollegiate athletics programs shall be conducted in a manner designed to protect and enhance the . . . educational welfare of student-athletes. . . . Intercollegiate athletics programs shall be maintained as a vital component of the educational program and student-athletes shall be an integral part of the student body. . . . The admission, academic standing and academic progress of student-athletes shall be consistent with the policies and standards adopted by the institution for the student body in general.

The purpose of this article is not to take a position about the pros or cons of increasing commercialization in college athletics. It seems that the die is cast, and Myles Brand has spoken to the NCAA's position that commercialization can co-exist with a notion of educational primacy for student athletes. Although this position is perhaps a bit naïve in some ways, it is the authors' intent to take a micro-level look at some of the obstacles that may deter student athletes from achieving their academic potential once they have been admitted to a university. This article does not attempt to address the issues related to recruiting athletes and the common practice of admitting some student athletes who may not be fully qualified to attend college (Ridpath and others, 2007). This article does not deal with any of the incidents related to academic fraud. Nor does it deal with the student athlete who chooses to attend college only to facilitate his or her entry into the ranks of professional athletics and does not care about academic achievement or attaining a meaningful education. Rather, in looking at those who choose to be a student athlete in good faith, what are some of the issues that affect the academic achievement of student athletes, and what may facilitate provision of a "meaningful education" for student athletes?

The term *meaningful education* begs precise definition. However, one commentator described a "meaningful education" as the "intellectual development of students engaged in good faith in the educational process" (Widener, 1982, p. 470).

NEW DIRECTIONS FOR HIGHER EDUCATION • DOI: 10.1002/he

If the primary purpose for all students is to acquire an education, then the university must carefully consider its obligation to furnish a meaningful education. This is especially true for the student athlete who commonly faces the competing interests of the intercollegiate athletic and academic programs, such as time demands and conflicting schedules between practices and games and classes.

Despite the call for educational primacy by Brand and the statements embodied in the NCAA Manual, the reality is often far from the stated ideal. Obstacles that student athletes often face are discussed in the next section.

Specific Factors Affecting the "Meaningful Education" of Student Athletes

Time Demands. Despite NCAA regulations that ostensibly limit the time spent on athletic pursuits to twenty hours per week (2007–08 NCAA Division I Manual Bylaw 17.1.5.1.), a recent survey of twenty-one thousand college athletes revealed that many athletes spend considerably more time on their sport. "Major-college football players reported spending an average of 44.8 hours a week practicing, playing, or training for their sport, the survey found, with golfers, baseball players, and softball players not far behind" (Wolverton, 2008, p. A23).

The NCAA mandates that during season teams practice no more than twenty hours a week and no more than four hours a day, with a day off; however, these hours do not include traveling to games, treatment with the athletic trainer, and other time-consuming activities that are not in the countable time. Research supports that all sports, regardless of whether nonrevenue or revenue sports, "have significant time demands and other distractions that may inhibit persistence and graduation" (Ridpath and others, 2007, p. 59).

The time demands on intercollegiate athletes have often been discussed as having a negative effect on academic performance. In an early study, Maloney and McCormick (1992) concluded that a seasonal drop in the GPAs of collegiate athletes, especially in the revenue-producing sports of football and men's basketball, was related to the inordinate time demands during their seasons of participation.

In addition to the time commitment, one cannot discount the fatigue factor. After a strenuous practice or contest, there is little energy left to devote to academic pursuits. Athletes are tired and may often be injured, which affects their ability to focus on studying or attending class (Simons, Van Rheenen, and Covington, 1999).

Choice of Major. The same NCAA study cited above also presents some data on the choice of major: "One in five athletes says their sports participation has prevented them from choosing the major they wanted" (Wolverton, 2008, p. A23). Also, a study released at the 2007 NCAA Convention reported that almost one-third of Division I football and men's basketball players stated that athletics participation has prevented them from choosing the major they desired (Knobler, 2007).

A review of academic majors chosen by football players who competed in the 2002–03 bowl games demonstrated that there are widespread clusters of athletes in specific fields of study: "Whether or not they admit it, academic advisers sometimes steer athletes into specific courses and degree programs to make it easier for them to meet the NCAA's academic standards" (Suggs, 2003, p. A33).

Some have raised the concern that the increased academic standards under the Academic Progress Rate (APR) may have fostered increased channeling of athletes into "easy majors." Also, the NCAA changed its methodology for continuing eligibility not only by requiring student athletes to pass a particular number of credits corresponding to their class standing (freshman, sophomore, junior, or senior); now they must pass these credits toward a percentage of degree completion. This has stopped the prior practice of student athletes finishing their eligibility with enough credits but not attaining a degree. However, now there is a trend of student athletes being placed in whatever is considered the "easiest" major. This trend, coupled with the onset of degree programs that are distance learning courses in which students may complete all required work via computer with no class attendance, has brought about another host of issues.

Negative Stereotypes and Academic Motivation. In a recent study of 538 college athletes, 33 percent reported that professors negatively perceive them and 59.1 percent said other students did so (Simons, Bosworth, Fujita, and Jensen, 2007). The comments made by professors and students reinforced the "dumb jock" stereotype and served to stigmatize and alienate student athletes. Student athletes who buy in to this negative stereotype may disengage from their academic obligations.

In October 2007, the Knight Commission held a Faculty Summit on Intercollegiate Athletics. At that meeting, the results of a survey of 2,071 faculty members at Division I-A institutions (now known as the NCAA's Football Bowl Subdivision) were disseminated. In regard to academic issues, it was disclosed that a majority of faculty members (61 percent) believe that athletes are motivated to earn their degree. However, this means that 39 percent have contrary opinions. Also, nearly a third (32 percent) of faculty surveyed believe that "some compromises with academic standards must be made to achieve athletics success in football and basketball" (Knight Foundation, Executive Summary Faculty Perceptions, 2007, p. 6).

In a survey conducted at a prominent Division I-A university, college students at that institution perceived that student athletes received special treatment by faculty members (Knapp, Rasmussen, and Barnhart, 2001). Further, only 23 percent of those surveyed agreed with the statement that "upon entering college, the primary goal of student athletes is to earn their degree" (Knapp, Rasmussen, and Barnhart, 2001, p. 98).

Simons and colleagues (1999) also commented on the relationship between self-worth and academic motivation. They found that the athletes who had lower academic self-worth were likely to put in less academic effort and "rationalize this reduced academic effort by employing self-handicapping excuses along with the claim that they are being exploited by the university" (p. 159).

The Culture of the Team. It is clear that a college coach assumes an important role in a student athlete's life. Coaches can have a major impact on all facets of their student athletes' lives, with the influence extending well beyond the playing field or gymnasium. With regard to the college athlete, Davis (1991, pp. 787–788) stated that schools often control the daily lives of athletes, and in so doing "a relationship of trust and dependence often develops that is not present in the relationship between lay students and universities."

In view of the degree of control and influence possessed by a coach, it is critical that the coach foster a culture of academic importance. Adler and Adler's seminal book (1991) on the role identity of athletes and the phenomenon of role engulfment clearly showed that the attitude of a coach relative to the importance of academic achievement was a critical factor in whether athletes viewed academics as important and whether they succeeded academically.

Some Strategies for Improving the Quality of the Academic Experience for Student Athletes

There is definitely an inherent tension between the goals of academic excellence and the goals of academic success for student athletes. Many commentators choose to view this tension as inherently irreconcilable and thus call for abolition of the current system of Division I athletics. However, there is not necessarily a philosophical divide that makes achievement of both ends unattainable; rather, it is the essential balance placed by each educational institution that goes to whether the tension can be managed.

Therefore, before any strategies can be successfully implemented, *all* members of an athletic department must be committed to core values that foster an environment in which a meaningful education for student athletes is truly desired. The academic achievement of student athletes must be valued as much as athletic excellence. If not, the strategies described here will be certain to fail for lack of commitment to the underlying principle of academic success.

Everyone in the athletic department has a role to play in insuring academic success. There must be congruence and a commitment to this core value of academic excellence in every facet of the athletics program. Without a holistic perspective and common values, these strategies cannot succeed.

The Coach's Role. The influence of coaches on their student athletes is critical. It is very important that the culture of the athletics department stress the role that coaches can and should play in encouraging academic excellence by their student athletes. This must be more than lip service; coaches often perceive (and realistically so) that their livelihood depends on their won-lost record and is not related in any meaningful way to the academic achievement of their student athletes.

This culture of academic excellence must be embraced by all in the athletic department. It cannot be accomplished by having only those who work in academic support or CHAMPS/Life Skills programs as facilitators. No one has greater influence than a coach upon the student athlete's motivation and dedication to do well academically. Thus, coaches must be hired who will emphasize academics as well as athletic prowess. Moreover, coaches must be rewarded for doing the right thing in terms of student athletes' academic success. Bonus provisions with some substantial economic incentives should be incorporated into the employment contracts of coaches. It does no good to state that academics are valued and yet give little or no incentive to coaches to actually focus on this aspect of their employment. Most Division I-A coaching contracts in the revenue-producing sports of football and men's basketball have minimal rewards for the academic achievements of student athletes compared to the extensive bonus provisions for number of wins, conference titles, bowl game appearances, and so on.

As discussed earlier, there are three specific ways in which coaches can have a positive impact. First, coaches need to allow a balance between team obligations and academics so that student athletes have a realistic amount of time to devote to their studies. No matter what the motivation level of the student athlete is, there must be time in which the student athlete is relatively rested and alert to devote to academic pursuits. This is very difficult to implement because coaches and players are often so single-minded in the pursuit of athletic excellence, and the time expectations, as was already discussed, are quite demanding. However, it is well accepted in the realm of sports psychology that there is not always a positive relationship between amount of practice time and performance. Sport psychologists should be consulted to help coaches *optimize* their practice time, not just maximize it.

Second, coaches should assist players psychologically to view their role as truly student athletes and not just athletes. If students come to view their self-worth as tied exclusively to their exploits on the playing field or in the arena, they will neglect their academic role and focus only on their athletic role, to the detriment of academic pursuits. Student athletes are quite attentive to the messages that coaches send, whether overt or subtle. If there is a true commitment to academic excellence, coaches can send a strong message about the importance of doing well in the classroom. This would include discussing the consequences of student athletes missing class or of poor academic performance. Just as coaches set goals for all other aspects of the sport, this should be a goal set for the team. It should also include a thorough education with student athletes about the remote likelihood of their being able to pursue a playing career in professional sports.

Third, coaches should interact with athletic department support staff to help facilitate student athlete academic achievement. The goal should be to facilitate a student athlete's ability to obtain a quality education, not just to keep a student athlete eligible for competition. As has already been noted, some student athletes feel they have had to compromise on the choice of major because of athletics. Many athletes may have felt they were channeled into a course of study that might have facilitated their likelihood to get good grades but at the expense of any real interest in the major. In some cases, the major may not have any real value in achieving career goals.

This is also a difficult issue because some majors are more demanding in terms of rigor and time. Some courses of study may require lab classes that can conflict with team practice times. It is impermissible for a student athlete to miss class for practice, so coaches must be diligent (especially if they have a larger number of upperclassmen) to pick a practice time that is available for all. Consequently, coaches schedule very early morning or very late practice to accommodate these issues. Either way, this can make it quite difficult for a student athlete in terms of getting enough sleep. There may be occasions when academic concerns directly conflict with athletic concerns. The resolution of these conflicts turns directly on the culture of the athletic department and what is really valued. Most student athletes will not go on to a career in professional athletics, so a quality education is paramount in preparing the student to meet the challenges of life and work.

With the change in the NCAA rules regarding graduation rate and the new academic progress rate (2007–08 Division I Manual, Bylaw 23), coaches will be required to face the consequences if their student athletes do not graduate. With this increased pressure, it will be imperative that the individuals who are discussed here play a key role in ensuring integrity and commitment to academics.

The Faculty Role.   The literature suggests that many faculty view student athletes as less than capable academically, especially those who participate in revenue-producing sports. They may stigmatize student athletes, which can lead to increasing alienation of student athletes from their academic endeavors.

Faculty may also not fully understand issues related to athletics and be disconnected from issues regarding college sports. This finding is particularly interesting because those surveyed in the Knight Commission Study on Faculty Perceptions (2007) included faculty who were involved in governance on campus:

"Concerning academic issues, more than half (53%) have no opinion about their satisfaction with coaches' roles in the admissions process; nearly half (49%) do not know if a faculty committee on campus regularly monitors the educational soundness of athletes' programs of study; 40 percent have no opinion about the academic standards on their campus that guide admission decision in football and basketball" (Executive Summary, Faculty Perceptions, 2007, p. 4).

The athletic department should join with faculty governance to showcase the academic achievements of student athletes and explain to faculty how athletic department personnel (including coaches) support and value the goal of academic achievement: "College staff and faculty, with the cooperation of the athletic department, need to be more involved in the lives of student athletes" (Simons, Van Rheenen, and Covington, 1999, p. 160).

Faculty should be educated about the time demands and pressures that all student athletes experience—with a clear message from athletics, however, that these pressures do not mean that student athletes are seeking a reduction in the expectations of achievement in classes. This opportunity is typically afforded through the Faculty Athletic Committee, in conjunction with the Faculty Athletic Representative (FAR). However, meeting with this committee and the FAR does not usually translate to other faculty members' acceptance or understanding of the student athletes' obstacles. The athletics department should not just "expect" faculty to agree to multiple class absences by student athletes. There should be a discussion with faculty about the student athletes' need to miss some classes, but with a clear understanding that this does not mean a dispensation from meeting all the demands of the class.

Further, the athletic department should educate all student athletes regarding the importance of communication with the faculty, being on time, sitting in the front row, and participating in class. Additionally, the athletic department should look for opportunities to bring faculty into the athletic program as faculty guest coaches or as honored guests. Having a banquet to celebrate student athletes who have achieved the Athletic Director's Honor Roll and inviting faculty mentors is also a good way to bring the two worlds together to better understand each other's viewpoints and priorities.

The Role of Student Government.   It is not just faculty who may stigmatize student athletes. As discussed earlier, the student perception of the student athlete may also be negative regarding academics. Students who are not athletes may feel at times that student athletes have privileges that are unfair and unwarranted, such as priority registration, because most students do not understand the time demands of participation and the strict eligibility requirements placed on student athletes by the NCAA.

Therefore, the Student Athlete Advisory Committee (SAAC) should try to cooperate with student government to correct misinformation or perceptions by students regarding athletics generally and regarding the role of academics in the lives of student athletes. Although the time for campus involvement outside of athletics may be limited, student athletes who are leaders should be encouraged to seek office in student government.

CHAMPS Life Skills Program and Athletic Academic Support Systems. Although some institutions have brought the Academic Support Systems and CHAMPS (Challenging Athletes' Minds for Personal Success) Life Skills Programs together, others have not. There has been a recent trend to transfer oversight of Athletic Academic Support Services back to the main campus to ensure that the reporting lines of academic staff are not negatively influenced by the other goals of the athletic department. The ideal situation is one that maximizes institutional control for all involved.

The CHAMPS Life Skills Program is designed to develop the whole student athlete in five commitment areas: personal, career, service, athletic, and academics. This program allows a total support system around student athletes to help them succeed both in the classroom and in their sport. The NCAA offers various grants that can be used to support this programming, but the commitment of each institution to developing the whole student athlete is vital. This commitment involves financial and personnel resources, and possibly facilities. This programming helps student athletes who face an atypical lifestyle with many time demands and challenges.

Regardless of the configuration of the academic support system for student athletes, it must include academic advisors who not only can properly advise on curriculum issues but also ensure NCAA eligibility is attained. This department within athletics should make available study hall, tutoring, and computer labs, and have the on-campus linkages for providing disability testing and assistance. The core value of academic excellence must drive decisions when conflict arises.

Academic advisors, CHAMPS Life Skills coordinators, and faculty may often feel puzzled in watching a student athlete who is motivated to do whatever it takes to be the best athlete then settle for mediocrity in the classroom, but it may be a matter of altering the student athlete's motivational style. The motivation of the student athlete is a critical factor in achieving academic success. A recent article by Curtis (2006) suggests that we should encourage the academic success of student athletes by modifying their goal orientation in the classroom from the student athlete's usual ego orientation to one of task orientation. Curtis notes that student athletes have been successful in athletics because they have used an ego orientation, which is dependent on superiority over others as a valuable model. However, the classroom is not an appropriate setting for ego orientation; task orientation, which focuses on success as a measure of internal competence, is a more apt model for the classroom. If student athletes retain their ego orientation for the classroom, Curtis asserts, they may become frustrated by a lack of direct competitive reference and the inability to choose appropriate goals. Therefore Curtis urges academic advisors to recognize this issue and try to teach student athletes to adopt a task orientation and thus modify how they perceive goal setting in the classroom, leading to more success in academic endeavors. Kane and Dale (2006) also found that motivating factors including self-efficacy and goal-orientation related to the academic achievement of student athletes.

NEW DIRECTIONS FOR HIGHER EDUCATION • DOI: 10.1002/he

A specific course focused on learning strategies may also be helpful in assisting at-risk student athletes. Tebbe and Petrie (2006) found that a learning strategies course, which addressed "fundamental cognitive and academic strategies that the student athletes may have been lacking" (p. 14), was helpful in managing anxiety, focusing attention, comprehending new information, applying test-taking strategies, and managing time. In this study, at-risk student athletes who took this course performed as well in their first and second freshman semesters as the student athletes who entered under normal admissions criteria.

Conclusion

It is quite clear that if influential role models (coaches, athletic staff, faculty) do not care how the student athlete performs academically, the student athlete's academic success will suffer. It is also clear that there are many strategies that can be implemented to help student athletes in their quest for a meaningful education. Thus educational institutions have the task of balancing the need for winning and having profitable athletic programs with maintaining the core value of academic success.

This balance is achievable if all parties are committed to academic success. The constituencies identified here all have an important role in nurturing and assisting the student athlete to achieve a meaningful education, which ultimately translates into these students' success beyond college as well.

References

Adler, P. A., and Adler, P. *Backboards and Blackboards: College Athletes and Role Engulfment.* New York: Columbia University Press, 1991.
Benford, R. D. "The College Sports Reform Movement: Reframing the 'Edutainment Industry.'" *Sociological Quarterly,* 2007, *48,* 1–28.
Brand, M. "The Principles of Intercollegiate Athletics." NCAA State of the Association Address, NCAA Annual Conference, January 7, 2006. Retrieved from http://www2.ncaa.org/portal/media_and_events/pressroom/2006/January/20060107.
Curtis, T. R. "Encouraging Student-Athletes' Academic Success Through Task Orientation Goal-Setting." *Journal of College and Character,* 2006, 7(3), 1–5.
Davis, T. "An Absence of Good Faith: Defining a University's Educational Obligation to Student-Athletes". *Houston Law Review,* 1991, *28,* 743–790.
Duderstadt, J. J. *Intercollegiate Athletics and the American University: A University President's Perspective.* Ann Arbor: University of Michigan Press, 2000.
Eitzen, D. S. "Slaves of Big-Time College Sports." *USA Today,* Sept. 2000, pp. 26–30.
Kane, T. R., and Dale, L. R. "Motivational Factors That Facilitate Student-Athlete Academic Achievement." *Academic Athletic Journal,* 2006, 19(1), 24–37.
Knapp, T. J., Rasmussen, C., and Barnhart, R. K. "What College Students Say About Intercollegiate Athletics: A Survey of Attitudes and Beliefs." *College Student Journal,* 2001, *35*(1), 96–100.
Knight Foundation Commission on Intercollegiate Athletics. *Reports of the Knight Foundation Commission on Intercollegiate Athletics.* Charlotte, N.C.: Knight Foundation, 1991, 1993.
Knight Foundation Commission on Intercollegiate Athletics. *A Call to Action: Reconnecting College Sports and Higher Education.* Charlotte, N.C.: Knight Foundation, 2001.

Knight Foundation Commission on Intercollegiate Athletics. *Executive Summary Faculty Perceptions of Intercollegiate Athletics Survey.* Charlotte, N.C.: Knight Foundation, Oct. 15, 2007.

Knobler, M. "Athletes Choose Majors to Accommodate Sports." *Atlanta Journal-Constitution.* Jan. 7, 2007. Retrieved from http://www.ajc.com/sports/content/sports/stories/2007/01/06/0107ncaa.html.

Maloney, M. T., and McCormick, R. E. "An Examination of the Role That Intercollegiate Athletic Participation Plays in Academic Achievement." *Journal of Human Resources,* 1992, 28(3), 555–570.

National Collegiate Athletic Association (2007–08) NCAA Division I Manual. Indianapolis: NCAA.

National Collegiate Athletic Association. "CHAMPS/Life Skills Program." Retrieved from http://www.ncaa.org/wps/portal/!ut/p/kcxml/04_Sj9SPykssy0xPLMnMz0vM0Y_QjzKL N4g38nYBSYGYxqb6kWhCjggRX4_83FSgeKQ5UMA0NFQ_Kic1PTG5Uj9Y31s_QL8 gNzSiPN9REQD6aqlp/delta/base64xml/L0lDU0lKTTd1aUNTWS9vQW9RQUFJUWd TQUFZeGpHTVl4V1U21BISEvNEpGaUNvMERyRTVST2dxTkM3OVl RZyEhLzdfMF81VVYvNjg2NTA2?WCM_PORTLET=PC_7_0_5UV_WCM&WCM_G LOBAL_CONTEXT=/wps/wcm/connect/NCAA/Academics%20and%20Athletes/CHA MPS%20%20Life%20Skills/.

Ridpath, B. D., and others. "Factors That Influence the Academic Performance of NCAA Division I Athletes." *SMART Journal,* 2007, 4(1), 59–83.

Sack, A. L. "Big-Time Athletics vs. Academic Values: It's a Rout." *Chronicle of Higher Education,* Jan. 26, 2001, pp. B7–B9.

Sack, A., and Staurowsky, E. *College Athletes for Hire: The Evolution and Legacy of the NCAA's Amateur Myth.* Westport, Conn.: Praeger, 1998.

Savage, H. J. *American College Athletics.* New York: Carnegie Foundation for the Advancement of Teaching, 1929.

Shulman, J., and Bowen, W. *The Game of Life: College Sports and Educational Values.* Princeton: Princeton University Press, 2001.

Simons, H. D., Bosworth, C., Fujita, S., and Jensen, M. "The Athlete Stigma in Higher Education." *College Student Journal,* 2007, 41(2), 251–273.

Simons, H. D., Van Rheenen, D., and Covington, M. V. "Academic Motivation and the Student Athlete." *Journal of College Student Development,* 1999, 40(2), 151–162.

Sperber, M. *Beer and Circus: How Big-Time Sport Is Crippling Undergraduate Education.* New York: Holt, 2000.

Suggs, W. "Jock Majors." *Chronicle of Higher Education,* Jan. 17, 2003, pp. A33–34.

Tebbe, C. M., and Petrie, T. A. "The Effectiveness of Learning Strategies Course on College Student-Athletes' Adjustment, Use of Learning Strategies, and Academic Performance." *Academic Athletic Journal,* 2006, 19(1), 1–22.

Widener, M. N. "Suits by Student-Athletes Against Colleges for Obstructing Educational Opportunity." *Arizona Law Review,* 1982, 24, 467–496.

Wolverton, B. "Athletes' Hours Renew Debate over College Sports." *Chronicle of Higher Education,* Jan. 25, 2008, pp. A1, A23.

Zimbalist, A. *Unpaid Professionals: Commercialism and Conflict in Big-time College Sport.* Princeton: Princeton University Press, 1999.

LINDA A. SHARP *is a professor of sports administration at the University of Northern Colorado. Much of her research relates to legal and ethical concerns in college sport.*

HOLLY K. SHEILLEY *is assistant athletic director for student development and championships at the University of Louisville.*

NEW DIRECTIONS FOR HIGHER EDUCATION • DOI: 10.1002/he

INDEX

115

NEW DIRECTIONS FOR HIGHER EDUCATION
Order Form
SUBSCRIPTIONS AND SINGLE ISSUES

DISCOUNTED BACK ISSUES:

Use this form to receive **20% off** all back issues of New Directions for Higher Education. All single issues priced at **$23.20** (normally $29.00). For a complete list of issues, please visit www.josseybass.com/go/ndhe.

TITLE	ISSUE NO.	ISBN
_____	_____	_____
_____	_____	_____
_____	_____	_____

Call 888-378-2537 or see mailing instructions below. When calling, mention the promotional code, JB7ND, to receive your discount.

SUBSCRIPTIONS: *(1 year, 4 issues)*

☐ New Order   ☐ Renewal

U.S.	☐ Individual: $85	☐ Institutional: $209
Canada/Mexico	☐ Individual: $85	☐ Institutional: $249
All Others	☐ Individual: $109	☐ Institutional: $283

Call 888-378-2537 or see mailing and pricing instructions below. Online subscriptions are available at www.interscience.wiley.com.

Copy or detach page and send to:
John Wiley & Sons, Journals Dept, 5th Floor
989 Market Street, San Francisco, CA 94103-1741

Order Form can also be faxed to: 888-481-2665

Issue/Subscription Amount: $ _____	**SHIPPING CHARGES:**		
Shipping Amount: $ _____	SURFACE	Domestic	Canadian
(for single issues only—subscription prices include shipping)	First Item	$5.00	$6.00
Total Amount: $ _____	Each Add'l Item	$3.00	$1.50

(No sales tax for U.S. subscriptions. Canadian residents, add GST for subscription orders. Individual rate subscriptions must be paid by personal check or credit card. Individual rate subscriptions may not be resold as library copies.)

☐ Payment enclosed (U.S. check or money order only. All payments must be in U.S. dollars.)

☐ VISA ☐ MC ☐ Amex # _____ Exp. Date _____

Card Holder Name _____ Card Issue # _____

Signature _____ Day Phone _____

☐ Bill Me (U.S. institutional orders only. Purchase order required.)

Purchase order # _____
                    Federal Tax ID13559302   GST 89102 8052

Name _____

Address _____

Phone _____ E-mail _____

JB7ND

NEW DIRECTIONS FOR HIGHER EDUCATION
IS NOW AVAILABLE ONLINE AT WILEY INTERSCIENCE

What is Wiley InterScience?

Wiley InterScience is the dynamic online content service from John Wiley & Sons delivering the full text of over 300 leading scientific, technical, medical, and professional journals, plus major reference works, the acclaimed *Current Protocols* laboratory manuals, and even the full text of select Wiley print books online.

What are some special features of Wiley InterScience?

Wiley InterScience Alerts is a service that delivers table of contents via e-mail for any journal available on Wiley InterScience as soon as a new issue is published online.

Early View is Wiley's exclusive service presenting individual articles online as soon as they are ready, even before the release of the compiled print issue. These articles are complete, peer-reviewed, and citable.

CrossRef is the innovative multi-publisher reference linking system enabling readers to move seamlessly from a reference in a journal article to the cited publication, typically located on a different server and published by a different publisher.

How can I access Wiley InterScience?

Visit http://www.interscience.wiley.com

Guest Users can browse Wiley InterScience for unrestricted access to journal Tables of Contents and Article Abstracts, or use the powerful search engine.

Registered Users are provided with a *Personal Home Page* to store and manage customized alerts, searches, and links to favorite journals and articles. Additionally, Registered Users can view free Online Sample Issues and preview selected material from major reference works.

Licensed Customers are entitled to access full-text journal articles in PDF, with select journals also offering full-text HTML.

How do I become an Authorized User?

Authorized Users are individuals authorized by a paying Customer to have access to the journals in Wiley InterScience. For example, a university that subscribes to Wiley journals is considered to be the Customer. Faculty, staff and students authorized by the university to have access to those journals in Wiley InterScience are Authorized Users. Users should contact their Library for information on which Wiley journals they have access to in Wiley InterScience.

ASK YOUR INSTITUTION ABOUT WILEY INTERSCIENCE TODAY!

Complete online access for your institution

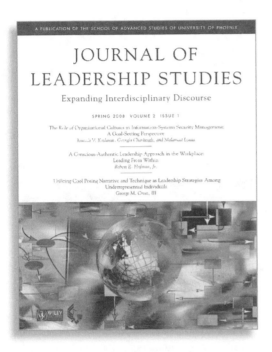

A PUBLICATION OF THE SCHOOL OF ADVANCED STUDIES OF UNIVERSITY OF PHOENIX

JOURNAL OF LEADERSHIP STUDIES

Expanding Interdisciplinary Discourse

SPRING 2008 VOLUME 2 ISSUE 1

The Role of Organizational Cultures in Information Systems Security Management:
A Goal-Setting Perspective
Jason V. Kaslanis, Georgia Charalambi, and Maksimal Louis

A Conscious-Authentic Leadership Approach in the Workplace:
Leading From Within
Robert E. Hofman, Jr.

Utilizing Cool Posing Narrative and Technique as Leadership Strategies Among
Underrepresented Individuals
George M. Cross, III

WILEY

Register for complimentary online access to *Journal of Leadership Studies* today!

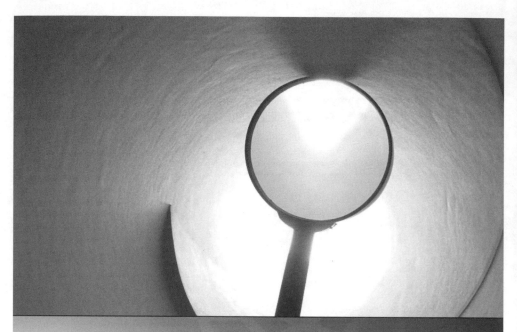

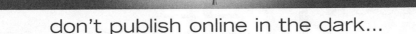